©2016 Tiffany Lee Gaston

All rights reserved. No part of this publication may be reproduced, distributed, or transmitted in any form or by any means, including photocopying, recording, or other electronic or mechanical methods, except in the case of brief quotations embodied in critical reviews and certain other noncommercial uses permitted by copyright law.

Cover Images Copyright 2015
James Patrick

MUH
Amanda Bland Artistry

Interior Design and Layout
James Rivers | Titan Media Marketing

ISBN: 978-1-942306-58-0
eISBN: 978-1-942306-59-7

Interior Book Images:
Lisa Hensley
Paul Buceta
Meggan Jacks
James Patrick

Printed By Printopya, LLC. Printopya.com

Printed in the United States of America

ACKNOWLEDGMENTS

To my loving husband John: Thank you for accepting me as I was, the young, hot-headed, know-it-all, that needed your gentle guidance to find my way out of a nightmare. You saw something in me I didn't yet see in myself.

Thank you for saving me. Because of your belief in me, I discovered belief in myself. Without your supportive nature, I could have never taken this leap of faith. Of all the many gifts you've graced me with in this lifetime, your kind heart and our three amazing children are unmatched.

I am grateful each day I wake up next to my best friend in this dream we've built together over the past 16 years. I love you more than words can express.

To my beautiful children, Rylie, Alexis and Davis, you are my reason for all I do. I want to make you proud and to teach you through my own mistakes and weaknesses, that you must never give up. I will always protect you, but I also realize I must give you the tools to become your own unique people.

Watching that unfold daily makes me more proud than anything I've ever accomplished. I'm not sure I want you to ever read this book, but should you stumble upon it one day, I hope you'll realize that although I made many mistakes in life, I have fought long and hard to make up for them.

To my friends and family, I've felt your love and compassion through all of life's twists and turns, and I know and appreciate that you've always wanted what was best for me, even when I may not have believed it.

I know I haven't always been easy, but I am grateful you stuck by my side. Thank you for always supporting me and for always keeping me grounded.

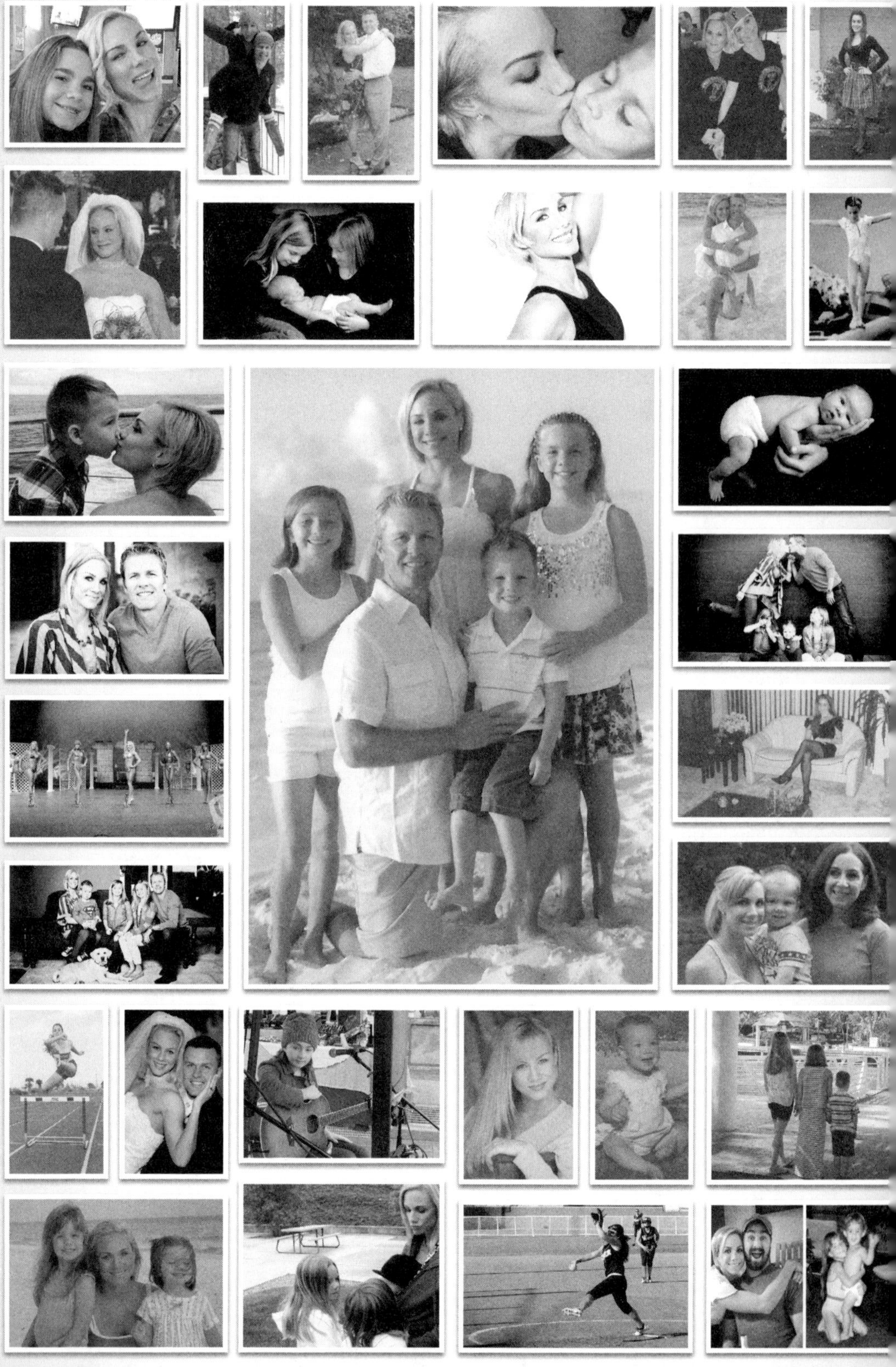

TABLE OF CHAOS

6	HAPPINESS IS A CHOICE
16	YOUNG BADASS
20	ANOREXIA
29	FAMILY MATTERS
42	SEX, DRUGS, AND ROCK AND ROLL
48	A WAY OUT
55	THE ABUSER
66	MY REBIRTH
80	BREAKING POINT
92	IN CONCLUSION
95	GIVING BACK
98	WHAT CAN YOU DO?
101	THE FIRST STEP
103	BEING TRUE TO YOURSELF
104	FINDING BALANCE
106	HEALTH IS WEALTH
108	FOOD IS NOT THE ENEMY
111	SET GOALS
112	LEARN TO DEAL WITH NEGATIVE EMOTIONS
113	STOP SELLING YOURSELF SHORT
116	YOU ARE A BEAUTIFUL BADASS
119	POST SCRIPT

HAPPINESS IS A CHOICE

TIFFANY LEE GASTON | FROM BROKEN TO BADASS

HAPPINESS IS A CHOICE

Have you ever misplaced something at the exact moment you really needed it? Doesn't it make you mad? I suppose the timing makes sense, because when you need something is when you'll certainly notice if it's not there, and because you need it *right then*, its disappearance can be completely maddening.

Car keys, for example. If you're at home playing with the kids or relaxing in the tub or watching TV or working out, the last thing you're concerned with are your keys. But when your appointment is in twenty minutes and you live thirty minutes away and you really wanted to stop for that latte, those missing keys can turn your calm into a raging cyclonic nightmare of WHERE THE FUCK ARE MY KEYS?!

Once the keys are found, always in the last place you look, (which also makes sense because why would they ever be where they are supposed to be?) calm is hopefully restored and you can focus on your NASCAR-like driving skills to get to where you need to be.

You may be running late, but at least you're in control.

Our fate is in our own hands. We are in the driver's seat of our own life.

But sometimes we lose things that are a little more difficult to find again. Sometimes we lose things that are harder to get back. Sometimes we lose who we are, and how do you go looking for that?

About eight years ago, I completely lost my sense of self. My identity. I woke up one day and felt like I was separate from who I had once been. I was not the person I had always thought myself to be. It was a strange sensation. I felt totally lost and out of sorts.

My identity wasn't misplaced or stolen. I had slowly given it away, bit by bit, piece by piece, without even realizing it, until I was not the person I wanted to be.

At 29 years old, a married mother of two little girls with a wonderful husband, I had everything I could possibly dream of and yet somehow I felt incomplete. Unfulfilled.

Yes, I know. First world problems, right?

But no matter how fortunate or unfortunate our circumstances, we are all just people, and every human being ever born has at one point experienced the same emotions, hopes, and dreams as every other human being. And that includes the same insecurities and fears, as well. It is what makes us human, what we all share, and how we deal with such things is what makes us happy, or unhappy, depending on those choices. As it turns out, no amount of money or material things can make you happy if you don't feel whole inside.

I was a lost soul and unsure of how I found myself in that position until I was finally able to face the sad reality that I had been living a lie. My choice to be a wife and mother were decisions I did not take lightly, but I allowed them to consume me until I no longer recognized myself.

Too much of anything can be unhealthy, and the idea that I had to fit into a particular mold and check off each and every box society dictated, caused me to bury myself within those roles. I waited until I truly felt we were ready to have children before making such a huge life decision. I wanted to feel that I was in a great place before bringing any children into the equation and in my mind, I did just that.

But I also faded into the background of my own life and lost all desire for what I once wanted so desperately. Don't misunderstand me; I love being a wife and mother. It is by far the most important and fulfilling thing I've ever done. But I wanted to do other things, too, and I no longer felt that same passion for those things.

When we lose our dreams, or just let them slip away, we lose a part of ourselves.

I began to slowly drift into depression. There was no big, life-changing event, no unexpected trauma, no earth-shattering crisis that led me there. It was a just a gradual loss of who I was and a slow decline into melancholy, something I never saw coming, but which was about to rock my world with the force of an oncoming freight train.

My life, as I knew it, was about to turn upside down.

Depression is something many people will experience at some point in their lives.

According to the National Institute of Mental Health,

> *"Mental disorders affect tens of millions of people each year, only about half of those affected receive treatment."*

Sometimes it passes quickly and sometimes it lingers. It can be as deep as the ocean or a brief, shallow dip into sadness. But the effects can be devastating if we don't recognize it and seek help, whether from friends, family or a professional. I had suffered briefly from post partum depression after my first born, but once my hormones regulated themselves, I was okay. This was different.

We all deserve to be happy, and we all want to be in the driver's seat of our own lives. For a perfectionist, being in control is extremely important, and I was spiraling out of control and hurtling down a very dark path.

I would have never imagined that everything I was so grateful for could leave me feeling so empty inside at the same time. Somehow, this strange dichotomy of emotions had become my reality. My husband, a hard-working, successful man, was often away during the early years of our marriage. He was working on behalf of our family, trying to build something amazing, but at the same time his absences made me feel alone and disconnected. As strange as it sounds, I felt like a single mother even though I had a loving husband.

Right or wrong, it was the way I felt at the time.

But instead of telling my husband all of that, I internalized my feelings. I kept them bottled up inside, which we all know is impossible to sustain.

At my core, I am a very passionate person and always have been, so I simply could not hold my emotions inside for long. You can guess what happened. I eventually exploded in anger and resentment, which of course is the worst way to communicate with someone you not only love and cherish, but whose help you desperately need. My mother had a short fuse when I was growing up, and that led to some fireworks between us, and I had vowed not to repeat that in my own life. But here I was, communicating in an unhealthy way, with raised voice and anger and all that comes with it. For me, this was a learned behavior.

My world was taking care of my babies, two precious little girls 16 months apart, but with my husband gone much of the time, I just felt alone. I married young, at 21, and who is totally formed at that age? I certainly was not.

I still had lots of growing to do, I realize looking back.

I was eager to have children a few years into our marriage. My babies were and are the love of my life, but they also drastically changed that life in ways I may not have been mature enough to handle. My exciting, fast-paced life became all about play dates, diapers, and naptime. I went from 60 to 0 in less than two years, and it was a *very* big adjustment.

And there were other issues too. I love my children more than anything, but I was still a young, vibrant woman, a sexual being with needs and desires that weren't, in my opinion, being properly addressed.

I should stop here for just a moment and say that this is not an uncommon concern for new mothers. Just because we give birth doesn't mean we've forgotten where it all began. I still wanted to feel sexy. I wanted my husband to find me as attractive as when we first met. He said all the right things, but it fell on deaf ears.

Despite a 50 pound weight gain with my first daughter and a 45 pound gain with the second, I lost the weight from each pregnancy rapidly due to my healthy lifestyle, but it wasn't enough for me. It wasn't that I had not returned to my former self physically; something internal had become disconnected. My wiring was definitely off.

And yes, I realize this is a two-way street. What part of marriage isn't?

My problem was that I just no longer felt as desirable as I once had, and that emotional void coupled with my husband's frequent absence and his intense work ethic caused my self-image to take quite a beating.

I felt like I was living in his shadow with two small children, and let me tell you, it can be awfully cold in the dark. That's one reason why people have affairs. They're looking for the warmth they aren't feeling at home.

And it was becoming very cold at home.

I was loved, but I wasn't *feeling loved*. And I didn't love myself too much, either. Giving all of myself to my young children and feeling like I was living in his shadow, gradually broke me down.

This is certainly not to lay all the blame on my husband. As I said before, we're all in the driver's seat of our own lives and that street we're sharing goes both ways. The constant giving to others and efforts to fit a certain expectation as a wife and mother left me feeling broken.

I wasn't happy, and he wasn't either.

If it sounds like a low point in my marriage, it most certainly was. Things got pretty bad between us. It was one of the most intensely difficult periods of my entire life.

It was also the best thing to ever happen to our marriage.

The fear of loss can be an eye opening experience. It's very true that we don't always appreciate what we have until it's gone, but if we're lucky, we get a chance to see what life would be like *before* we lose what's important, so that we can pull ourselves back from the abyss.

Both my husband and I realized we were at a crossroads, and the decisions we made from that moment forward would have very serious consequences.

The fear of losing what we had built together and what that meant for our children, allowed for some real soul searching.

We had reached our dark night of the soul, when every moment seemed like three in the morning. Late at night, when things are still, unquiet minds take over and emotions are heightened. And so it was with us. It was devastating to feel this way and not have the words to communicate how it was affecting me.

But as they say, things are always darkest before the dawn, which is why it's often better to sleep on things and take a second look in the cold light of day.

And so we did.

For us, it was a time for reflection, seven years deep into our marriage. A time to carefully consider what we meant to each other and where we were going. Most importantly, we were able to figure out all of that together.

We drew closer at our darkest moment. We took stock of our situation as partners and our willingness to work together, which is what makes a strong marriage to begin with. Neither of us had ever been more eager to take on a difficult task, which was the complete restructuring of our relationship. The foundation on which it was built, our deep love and respect for each other, was still solid.

But the structure needed work.

I began to remind myself daily:

"Love Conquers All."

The extreme personal growth we were able to ignite during such a difficult time, helped us form an even stronger bond than we'd shared before. By working through our pain and remorse, we formed a more perfect union, which continues to grow stronger each day, even now.

I am so grateful for that darkness, because it has made our light so much brighter. I am bathed in the light of my family every single day and have never felt more grateful for my three beautiful children and this amazing man who loves me with his entire being. I have never felt it more.

Overcoming that rough patch and strengthening our

marriage opened our eyes to having another child. John had always wanted a son. We tried for our third child and incredibly; we received the most amazing, perfect little boy I could ever imagine. I love all of my children with my entire being, but I think God gave us our son Davis to prove our love would continue to grow strong and show us we could overcome anything.

I can't imagine our world without him. The kindest, most affectionate, beautiful, baby boy, a tiny version of us both, entered this world on January 9, 2009. He was born and we were *reborn*.

Your struggles may or may not be similar to mine, but one thing's for sure: We will all experience good times and bad, but it's how we navigate through the storms that builds our character. How we meet life's challenges can be shared with others and lessons can be learned. This is why I'm sharing my personal story.

Not one of us experiences life in the exact same way, but that's what makes things interesting. Life is full of surprises. Sometimes the road we travel is filled with great blessings and sometimes, with tremendous heartbreak and tragedy. How we rise above the challenges is what builds our character and helps us to grow as human beings.

Tough times are unavoidable, but we need to meet them head on. As my personal experience shows, there's a lot of good that comes from the bad if we're open to the experience.

I now appreciate the value of all life's twists and turns, because even the tough times can lead us to where we need to be. I went from my lowest point to my greatest joy, because I made a choice to never give up on myself again.

It was no easy feat. I struggled to change my situation,

and truly believed I could. That seed of belief was all that I needed. Using my experiences to grow as an individual and also within my marriage, allowed me to become a better person. I have become a more confident, self-aware individual, as well as a better partner in crime.

Whether you have ever been in a similar situation, know someone who has, or are just curious about where I've been, sharing my story will have been worthwhile if even one person is enlightened by my journey.

I have increased my inner peace just by digging these experiences out of deep, dark suppression and sharing it with you now.

I have also relived much of the pain I once denied myself in an effort to block out my past and pretend it couldn't touch me. But I've learned that you must feel your pain if you are to grow from it. It will give you great satisfaction to get back up after you're knocked down. To claw your way back to where you once were and beyond. That is what makes a fighter.

Be a fighter!

Though there are days when it's painful to revisit some of what I'm about to share, I am healed on a deeper level because of the process. My tears now are tears of joy, because by embracing forgiveness and releasing anger, I allow my full value to be determined by no one other than me.

Take my hand as I walk you through my journey. To understand my strength, you must first understand my pain and weakness. I want to share with you the fire that forged the steel, and hopefully we'll grow even stronger together.

> *"I wake up today with strength in my heart and clarity in my mind." – Unknown*

YOUNG BADASS

TIFFANY LEE GASTON | FROM BROKEN TO BADASS

YOUNG BADASS

I've always had a bit of an attitude. A hot-headed, sarcastic, sassy, smart-mouthed chick whose words were faster than her filters. You never had to guess what I was thinking, because I'd just give it to you straight. Not that I'm proud of it, mind you. To be perfectly honest, I was kind of a bitch. I was once proud of that, but no longer.

Sometimes my attitude worked to my advantage and sometimes it did not, but it was a part of who I was before I learned to communicate better and become a more patient and kind-hearted person. I eventually learned to appreciate that words can hurt and leave irreparable damage to relationships if we fling them around too carelessly.

I always knew I was different; but sadly, there was a time when I somehow got it in my head that standing out was a bad thing. I've come to see individuality and independence as qualities to be admired, but as children, we often just want to fit in.

From the age of six, I was an athlete. Built on the frame of a competitive gymnast, which often did not go unnoticed. I was always small, compact, and muscular - built like a tiny brick shithouse. Bouncing from competitive gymnastics and dance as a child, to cross-country and track and field during high school. It seemed like I had never been without a goal or a desire to be better. I always had a competitive drive to excel, to win, to be the very best I could be in whatever I did. I really didn't know anything else.

I'm not sure where that internal drive came from, but being in competitive sports from an early age meant that I was always told I could "do it." Whatever "it" was, could be accomplished with hard work. Anything and everything was within my grasp as long as I really wanted it and went after it with everything I had. My parents told me so.

And that same drive applied not just to sports, but also to life. I was told I could be anything I wanted to be, and I believed it with my entire being.

As a competitive gymnast, my body was often a topic of discussion, which left me feeling very self-conscious when I was young. I'll never forget the time I was in a hardware store with my parents around the age of eight, and a middle-aged man commented how "awesome" my legs were.

He wasn't speaking to my parents though, which I guess might have been a more appropriate conversation. He was talking to me.

Think about how strange that would have been to a second grade girl. An adult that towered above me, leaned down, gave me a long, appraising look and commented on my body. Completely uncomfortable and I'm fairly certain I turned a shade of red I was unaware was even possible. Horrified was an understatement. I don't even recall how my parents responded, but that moment forever stayed with me.

All kids get used to awkward conversations with adults at family gatherings, but this was a perfect stranger. This wasn't my uncle asking me how I liked school or my grandmother asking about my current favorite hobbies, this was a man I'd never seen before telling me how "awesome" my legs looked.

And while this particular incident stuck out in my mind because of how creepy it was, my muscularity was often the topic of conversation, which really began to bother me over time. Eventually it became such a running theme in my life that I became exceedingly shy and introverted. I wanted to hide my body and just fit in with my friends.

Attention like that was the last thing I wanted.

It was ironic that I had worked so hard to excel in a sport that required me to perform alone in front of large crowds of people, but a single comment from a stranger outside that environment sent me on a downward spiral that would not only take me years to reverse, but quite literally threaten my life.

ANOREXIA

TIFFANY LEE GASTON | FROM BROKEN TO BADASS

ANOREXIA

By the time I was 12, fitting in had become an obsession. I recall being at a sleepover with my closest friends, and for some reason we weighed ourselves. Being the most muscular, I discovered I weighed more than my girlfriends. I was, however, one of the smallest, so you can see here how skewed my perception was.

That was extremely upsetting to me. It was just another way I wasn't "normal" and another reason I didn't fit in. I began to weigh myself constantly, tortured by the number on the scale. I couldn't shake the feeling that my weight was the key to everything. If I could just be like everybody else I would be happy, and that meant the number needed to come down. I needed to lose weight.

To get the number down, I made a decision that forever changed the course of my life. I discovered a new ability, something I was very good at, but it was not very good for me at all. I'd been taught that I could do anything I set my mind to and I believed it, and now I discovered the dark side of that belief.

I discovered I could starve myself.

It was a revelation, like a light bulb suddenly went off and I found the perfect solution to my problem, which of course should not have been a problem at all. I didn't need anyone's permission, I didn't have to buy anything, I didn't have to practice or take a class or get up early. All I needed was willpower, and that had never been a problem for me.

Not eating would make my body smaller. I wanted to shrink away. I wanted to disappear. It wasn't anything anyone told me, or something I learned in school or from a friend. I didn't know it had a name and I didn't realize it was an illness.

I was 12 years old and I hated my own body.

Why I thought disappearing would help me fit in with my friends is beyond my understanding. It makes no sense, I know. It sounds crazy, and that's part of the pathology. You don't see yourself as you really are and you don't recognize what you're doing is illogical. You don't see that it's harmful.

I made a choice to severely restrict my calories, and just like everything I ever set my mind to, I was very, very good at it.

Before social media and the Internet, magazines were the cultural obsessions of young girls, and I was no exception. I loved fashion and read every issue of Vogue and other fashion publications with the desire to look like the women I saw throughout their pages.

My mind was warped by images of what I thought beauty should be. I obsessed over Cindy Crawford, Helena Christensen, Nicki Taylor, and the other supermodels of the 90's. Imitating their poses, their walk, their makeup, became all consuming.

This is how messed up our society can be. We allow our kids, our young, impressionable children, to wallow in impossible imagery. They want to be like the images they see, and those images are simply not attainable by most people.

That goes for all our media, which rightly admires achievement, but then goes a step too far and glorifies it. Just as most little girls will never grow up to look like Giselle Bundchen, most little boys won't grow up to play football like Tom Brady, or play basketball like LeBron James.

Most young actors will not grow up to be movie stars, either. It's important to recognize achievement and honor talent and hard work, but it all needs to be put in perspective for each generation.

Children need the room to grow and find themselves and become the best person they can be, and that will not always be what they see portrayed in the media. Especially in the Kardashian era.

As a fitness model, I can tell you that the women you see in magazines and online are not as flawless as they appear, myself included. When you are unaware that some models have been Photoshopped into near alien-like versions of themselves, it's not fair to try to live up to that false expectation.

It's happened to me on the cover and inside of publications, and it always makes me furious. Publications are trying to appeal to certain demographics and occasionally they'll take a very heavy hand to an image in order to do just that. I've actually had my abs removed, something I work so hard for, simply because they are "intimidating" to the mainstream masses.

I never realized, at the age of 12, that wanting to be something I was not genetically predisposed to being was so very harmful to who I was meant to be.

My infatuation became an illness. Body Dysmorphic Disorder (BDD) is an obsession that an aspect of your body needs to be fixed, whether real or perceived. I'm sad to say I fell under its spell. I fell for the lies spoon fed to me through those magazines, although in time I would come to better understand the truth of a positive and healthy self-image. Sadly, not before damaging my own in the process.

In time, I learned that an eating disorder is so much more than just the desire to be skinny; it's a control mechanism. Being so young, I didn't have control over much in my world, but when I wasn't being watched I could control my calories, and that felt like power to me. Monitoring the scale several times a day was an obsession and a game, and I was winning the game as long as the number was decreasing.

I dropped to 85 pounds and wore baggy clothes to hide it. I told my parents I had eaten before they got home from work so I could skip dinner. I moved food around my plate if I couldn't avoid having dinner with my family to present the illusion I was eating. I threw away my school lunches. There were days I consumed only iceberg lettuce and water. It sounds strange now, but in my obsessed mind, it was a game and I was playing it well.

Eventually, there was no hiding my condition. I was simply too thin compared to what I had been. My face was gaunt and pale, my eyes sunken and lifeless, my energy non-existent.

My personality became even more withdrawn, and I lost friends because I avoided any unnecessary social situation. The fear of having to eat in front of other people was paralyzing, and my solution was to isolate myself.

I couldn't see that avoiding people during my quest to fit in, was self-defeating, and to be honest, fitting in became secondary to that number on the scale.

Everything was secondary to that number.

My shift in behavior and physical appearance finally became too much for my parents to take, and they threatened to hospitalize me. The vision of being force-fed was horrific to me, so much so, that I agreed to a compromise: Therapy.

I was extremely resistant and scared. Revealing my secret to others was part of the deal and I needed to do it, but at the time I only knew I didn't want to be forced to regain all the weight back I'd worked so hard to lose.

As reported by the National Eating Disorder Association, *"in the United States, 20 million women and 10 million men suffer from a clinically significant eating disorder at some time in their life, including anorexia nervosa, bulimia nervosa, binge eating disorder, or EDNOS."*

Isn't this an astounding statistic?

Even as I agreed to therapy, I was still trying to control the situation. I thought somehow I could beat the system.

After months of treatment, I was slowly recovering, but had a terrible aversion to my therapist. During one particular session, he told me there was actually nothing wrong with me, other than the fact I was just being a little "bitch" who "wanted control over my life."

Wow, did I just hear you correctly Dr. Asshole? This prick passed his boards? *You're fired!*

I think everyone strives to have control over their life, and as for the "bitch" part, it's completely unprofessional and counterproductive to deal with a patient in that way, particularly someone as confused as I was.

That was our last session.

My new therapist was far more professional, called me no names and began to help me understand why I had developed body dysmorphia and anorexia in the first place, which was exactly what I needed. By helping me discover the root cause of my issues, my new therapist allowed me to, yes, be in control of my own healing process. There's that control element again and I needed that.

This low point in my life gave way to a time of eye-opening discovery. I began to treat my body well. I wanted to make my parents proud and not feel the shame I felt I had brought upon them. I was learning how to develop a healthier body image, and began educating myself on proper nutrition. A huge part of that was redirecting my interest to fitness magazines and towards the women built more like me, not the tall, lanky supermodels I'd never look like.

These days, some of the publications I once read for my own inspiration, now feature my image on the cover and among their pages. I cried to the editor of Oxygen when I flew out to LA to shoot a feature spread for them in 2014. I literally broke down when I realized what a full circle moment that was for me.

I had shot for several well known fitness publications, yet somehow, the collaboration with Oxygen took me back to those moments as a young girl when I needed to see the strength of females as beautiful and connect with the healthy images among its pages. I needed to realize back then, that –

"I am powerful, I am strong, I am enough." TLG

I began to understand how muscularity related to weight, which had been a huge misunderstanding that fed my skewed perception in the first place.

The scale was removed from our home so I could no longer obsess over it, and from that day forward, I stood backwards on the scale at the doctor's office to avoid another downward spiral. My choice was to never look at the number because I knew I'd fixate on it once again.

To this day I rarely weigh myself, and when I do, I have no attachment to the number I see. I let go of that number to understand that I needed to feel good above all else. I needed to be healthy, and the number, whatever it was, was neither healthy nor unhealthy. It was just a number, nothing more. This is a tremendous accomplishment coming from where I had once been.

A huge part of healing was getting my mind right, which

took several years. I had tremendous hang-ups with going to a psychologist in the first place. My understanding of shrinks was that I was a freak if I needed one. I resented my parents for making me see one, and I was embarrassed for any of my friends to know. With all my internal struggles, the fact I needed to see a psychologist probably stayed with me the longest. That was a tough one to release.

Maybe that's a little bit of a control issue, huh?

I would later learn to better appreciate the benefits of therapy and never again looked at asking for help as some kind of weakness.

To the contrary, it often takes great strength to admit you need assistance and cannot do it alone. To humble yourself and ask for help is to recognize your truth. I wish I had not been so stubborn.

There is never shame in asking for help, only regret you didn't seek it sooner.

We're all a work in progress until the day we leave this earth, and control is one issue I'm constantly working on. When to hold onto it and when to let it go.

On the other hand, I've always had tremendous drive and creative energy, though I haven't always been grateful for the gift. I haven't always known what to do with all that physical ambition, but luckily I've been able to direct it into health and fitness.

Though not a religious person, I am most definitely spiritual. I have always felt protected and feel that there has always been something out there watching over me. I've stopped in my tracks and taken a new direction many times when I've been open to the learning the lesson.

Because of my drive and this feeling of protection,

nothing has ever felt of limits to me. I've always gone after everything I've ever wanted. I realize not everyone feels this way and I know how fortunate I am in that regard. It's my hope that others can find the same drive and confidence within themselves in order to become the best they can be.

I was always told, that because of my looks, things would come easily to me and in many instances that has been true.

In the instances when it did not, I wanted it all the more. I have always tried to see past what was right in front of me and imagine something bigger, something more to reach for, always striving to realize my dreams. I've always known there was so much out there for me to reach out and grab if I was willing to put in the work.

> *Passion is an irrefutable fire that burns within you for that which you are drawn. How sad it would be to never get to dance among those flames." – TLG*

But I've also had my share of hardships. There has been a lot of pain on my journey, too. Pain I have shared with very few until now. I have many scars, but I choose to see them as beautiful, because my scars have led me to a better place.

No one is only the person they appear to be on the surface; there is always a deeper story to be told.

This is mine.

These are my beautiful scars.

FAMILY MATTERS

I was the first-born child of hard working, middle class parents, brought into the world in Ft. Lauderdale, Florida on May 19, 1978, the height of its reputation as the U.S. capital of spring break madness. I grew up near the beach, though in retrospect, it seems we never did visit it much. We lived in a small, humble home and my mom stayed home with us in the early years, while my father worked full-time to provide all that we needed.

My parents were fairly young when they had me, in their mid-twenties, and I was an only child for the first five years of my life. I think long after my mother had Casey, I still behaved as such regardless. My mother suffered a miscarriage before having my brother, which widened the gap between us and also kept us apart emotionally.

I always felt having a sibling closer in age might've lent itself to a closer relationship, but that was not how things worked out. As adults, however, we are far closer than we ever were as kids. It's a nice feeling to observe a relationship grow stronger where it had not once been. I think time, life lessons, and maturity on both sides, played a large role in that outcome for us.

After getting us off to school, my mother went back to work. It was a mixed marriage, and by that I mean a white collar/blue collar type arrangement. My mother was clerical, always in an office and often the office manager, which was a good job for her since she was highly organized and enjoyed telling people what to do from time to time. I got a lot of that as a rebellious teenager, which I guess is par for the course with mothers and daughters. Having my own daughters entering their teenage years, I'm getting my own healthy dose of that now.

You know what they say about karma, she can be quite a bitch!

My father has been a transmission mechanic for forty years now, which suited his friendly, down-to-earth personality quite well. Like bartenders, mechanics naturally become good listeners to all kinds of people with all kinds of problems, and the best ones are as good with their ears as they are with their hands.

My dad has always been the handiest man around, sadly putting my own husband to shame in that department, though he'll never really own it. As my husband prefers to say, "I just don't want to spend my free time doing those things, I'd rather hire someone."

I giggle to myself and know my daddy could fix it if he lived closer.

My dad loves to tell a good story, but he is also a great listener. He was often the good cop in that well-known scenario, since I needed my share of policing during my formative years. But the good cop cannot succeed without the bad cop, and looking back with hindsight, I can see that my parents worked very well together to provide an amazing upbringing. They were simple people who lived modestly, never beyond their means, but saved well and always managed to provide my brother and I whatever we needed.

As I mentioned, my younger brother Casey came along five years after me, so I naturally felt protective of him from the very beginning. He was always the artistic one, from his artwork to photography to the guitar.

Since I grew up in competitive sports, I was always more driven than he was. He probably thought of me as the bossy older sister, but I saw that as part of my job. I was fiercely protective of my little brother because no one got to push him around him except me!

My mother told me that when Casey was a newborn, she was heading out to get the mail and distinctly told me, "Do not touch the baby Tiffany." In the midst of playing with my Barbies, I mumbled "okay," but when she returned, my baby brother had been moved in his crib onto his tummy and flipped around. I claimed I had nothing to do with it – clearly I was being a little shit. My brother had become my new little toy.

I took on a motherly role with him, likely because of our age gap and my pride in having first-born status. One thing is for certain, whether you are my blood or not, if I care for you, I'm in your corner and will always have your back.

I imagine this type of family dynamic is fairly common with our differences in age and sensibility. The oldest child often will assume certain responsibilities for a younger sibling; especially us type A's. But my attitude was always motivated by love, at least in my mind. I tried to look out for him, all the while feeling protective, yet hoping he'd someday discover the confidence to become successful and happy on his own.

Because of my father's job, he often came across used luxury cars we couldn't otherwise afford. I learned to drive in an S Class Jaguar, although I remember being highly embarrassed by it at the time. Most of my friend's parents didn't have cars like that.

But even though he brought home lots of cool cars, the first car I could call my own was an inexpensive and relatively uncool red Chevy Berretta, although let's be real – when you're in high school you want any car you can get your hands on. I was so eager to have my freedom, though completely unaware of what I'd do with it at that time.

My parents bought the car, but insisted I get a job to pay for gas and insurance, which taught me the responsibility of ownership. My very first job was in a local movie theater and I would also clean my grandparents' condo (on my mother's side) every other Saturday. I had lots of pride over earning my own money, which has always been important to me, unlike many of the bratty kids I went to school with.

Prior to having my own car, I daydreamed about all of the newfound freedom I would have. I considered visiting my father's parents, who lived just one town away. Seems sensible for a young girl just getting her license and a car, except that I hadn't seen them in over four years!

Growing up, my father's mother, Grandma Betty, was completely controlling of her husband, Papa Will. Over the years and beginning very early in their marriage, my mother felt the same behaviors towards my dad, which rightfully irritated her to no end. It would seem her mother-in-law could never really cut the cord.

My understanding has always been that she was terrific with us kids, but that same warmth wasn't always extended to my mother during much of their marriage. Her malicious behavior and intent was quite evident over the years, and it began to wear upon my parent's relationship. I was unaware of it at the time, as my parents seemed to deal with it behind closed doors. I had not yet seen anyone make much of a deal about her controlling ways.

I'd often spend the night at their home. I remember Grandma Betty taking me to the corner drugstore and letting me pick out every color nail polish and type of candy I wanted. I was still an only child back then before Casey came along and cramped my style.

Grandma Betty worked as the head cook and kitchen manager in a local elementary school for many years, bossing

TIFFANY LEE GASTON | FAMILY MATTERS

everyone around just like with her husband. She always had a surplus of Jell-O Pudding Pops, mini ice cream cups and whatever else she'd snag from the school kitchen in a spare freezer at her home and we helped ourselves to whatever we liked. She would make giant batches of the best Chex Mix I'd ever tasted and I always thought she was a great cook. I still remember the giant round Tupperware she'd store it in. Back then I didn't have a care in the world; everything was just dandy. We always had a great time with them and felt very loved.

Then one day, it all ended abruptly.

It was almost Christmas. I was 11 and my brother was 6. There was a situation of some sort and my dad finally took a stand for my mother in a way he hadn't before.

There was a big blowout and that year we didn't see our grandparents on Christmas Day as we always had before. We were told Papa Will would be coming over separately without Grandma Betty to deliver our gifts. He did, claiming he was sorry for the tension, but that he was the one that had to "live with her" so he was trying to keep the peace. I could feel how somber the room was even at that young, naive age. His tail was between his legs, unwilling to stray from her uncompromising orders. Papa Will seemed so cold and disconnected towards all of us, a side I'd never seen of him until that point.

Our other grandparents were present and witnessed his sad disposition as well. My Grandpa Jules sat on a barstool in the kitchen beside Papa Will and with sadness in his eyes, told him this was an unfair predicament she had put him in and that he needed to take a stand. Again, he reiterated this was his life and if he wanted smooth waters, he wouldn't be the one to create the waves.

My mom's parents had certainly been on the receiving

end of her toxic behavior and jealousy over the years. Many weekends, we'd have sleepovers at their home, just as we did my father's parents, however, this would create jealousy that wouldn't go unvoiced. It was always a tug of war with her and no one could ever win if they didn't play by her rules.

I believe everyone saw it, except the kids, and they all learned how to deal with her until they could no longer allow her to get away with it. I can't imagine the hell my Papa Will must have lived in, but as an adult, I can appreciate that it was entirely a choice he made. Others do not control us unless we allow it. I myself have tolerated the same and it was no one's fault but my own.

Despite a longtime estranged relationship, my father has since reconnected with his dad and they now speak nearly every day. I'd say the catalyst was the passing of his mom a few years ago. I'm grateful for the healing place they've evolved to, but I can't help but feel sad for all the years that were lost.

My father flew home to Florida from Atlanta when he learned his mother was failing, and as he sat at her hospital bedside, she finally let go of control. I hope somehow in those final moments my father forgave her, but I know it's a very personal battle he fought for many years.

As an adult with children of my own, I've still never had any desire to reconnect with Papa Will. Even at 16, I often envisioned driving to their home and knocking on the front door. I wondered if they'd recognize me, what I'd say to them, if it really even mattered. I was always told it was my choice to have a relationship with them, which I truly respect my mother for. She has always acknowledged that was a decision for her children to make all their own.

It was the strong resentment I harbored for all of those years that kept me away. I lost respect for my grandmother upon learning how she treated my mother and the resentment I harbored towards Papa Will for standing by her, was not something I could forget.

I've often questioned how grandparents could cut off grandchildren in the midst of an issue with their parents. What did it even have to do with Casey and me? Why were we caught in the middle? Innocent bystanders of the ridiculous control my grandmother aimed to execute over all the men in her life. I'd think to myself, *If you could simply cut off your grandkids because of tension between yourself and my mother, than you can go fuck yourself if you think I'm reaching out to you.*

It is very unfortunate that he is not part of my life and has missed out so much due to his own choices. I wonder if he has any regrets. Having several great-grandchildren he will never have the privilege of knowing is a choice he made. I've always cherished the close relationship I have with my 92-year-old Grandma Mimi, my mom's mom. Though my Grandpa Jules passed away over 15 years ago, he was also an amazing, kind-hearted spirit that I always felt such love from and for whom my second child carries his namesake.

I'll always be proud of my dad for standing up for my mom that very sad Christmas morning, and knowing full well what he was in for. I respect him so much for what he did and I've always known the sorrow he must've buried deep inside for having lost his mother simply because he took that stand.

I hope he was able to communicate some of that to her, while at her bedside as she passed. Though we have never had many discussions about it, I hope he has given himself the gift of forgiveness.

Throughout high school, I witnessed many kids allowing life to just happen to them. They floated along, always complaining about their situation, yet never doing a damn thing to change it.

Sadly, today I still see many adults complain about their circumstances, but continue to live their lives on repeat. I was aware of that type of behavior from an early age, because in competitive sports, even with coaches that push you, you still have to take responsibility for your own training when they are not around.

At the end of the day, if you're an athlete, no one pushes you harder than you push yourself. When you are doing the things that are necessary to make it to the next level, even when no one is watching, that's what makes a champion and I've always believed as such. So when I saw other kids who lacked the confidence to go after their dreams, I knew I didn't want that for myself.

I am a firm believer in building your own self-confidence and not relying on others for it. That way, if you're unhappy in your life, you'll be better equipped to do something about it, even when times are tough. Sometimes, all we have is blind faith and we must take a leap, rather than sitting in comfort and complacency, silently watching from the sidelines.

Sometimes happiness comes naturally, but sometimes it takes a lot of hard work. And just like all success, there can be a lot of blood, sweat and tears on the way up. But if the goal is your own happiness and self-fulfillment, it will all be worth it. That has always been my motivation above anything else. It's nice to have your parents look at you and beam with pride, but to maintain a pride within yourself for accomplishing your goals, is unlike anything else.

I could use my mother as an example of this. She's very strong-willed and opinionated (sounds like someone I know) and excelled in school, graduating early and attending Oxford. She backpacked through Europe as a young woman, did her fair share of drugs, but still ended up a wife and mother, both my confidant and my disciplinarian. She has always been honest with me about her past, but with no excuses.

When I was 15, she asked me if I'd ever smoked pot. I told her I had, but that I didn't like it, which was a total lie. The truth was, I loved getting high. Pot was an escape from the problems of my world like I had never known.

What I didn't know at the time, was that I have an addictive personality. But back then, everybody was smoking pot, and while that's never an excuse to do something stupid, it's a pretty common reason that goes back to that whole conformity thing. I wanted to fit in and I enjoyed the escape.

When I lied to my mother about my distaste for marijuana, she looked me straight in the eye, as if she was appraising my veracity, and murmured, "hmm." I'm sure she could see right through me, but the conversation changed and we didn't speak about it again. I'm sure she knew I would never admit the truth, and as a mother with a willful teenage daughter, you have to pick your battles. And we definitely had our battles.

I struggle to imagine her as the carefree, hippie-type in her youth, although I know from experience that marriage and motherhood can change things pretty drastically. Of course I've only known her as my mother, but fortunately I've also seen the hysterically funny and sarcastic side she doesn't always show the outside world.

In many ways she can be rather shy and introverted, although in her profession she's managed well over a hundred people at a time and is very professional and hard working.

I suppose she's always been a little bit of an enigma to me. Her intelligence and wit are sharp and focused, sometimes even aimed at me. But she is who she is, her own person who definitely showed me that I could do whatever I set my mind to, even if she didn't always agree with what that was. I've only ever felt support and love from her.

I'll never forget a moment of mindless conversation in the car with her when I was about ten years old. I have long since forgotten what we'd been talking about, but whatever it was, she had become really fired up over it. I recall her turning to me in the passenger's seat and blurting out in anger, "TIFFANY, DON'T YOU EVER TAKE SHIT FROM ANYONE!"

I can still see her face and hear the distinct tone in her voice. I couldn't help but to laugh at first, likely because it was funny to hear her swear, but I quickly realized she was deadly serious. I immediately stifled my giggles, attempted to keep a straight face, and muttered, "Okay mom."

She looked at me for a moment as if to gauge my level of actual understanding, and either decided to drop the subject or was satisfied that she'd gotten through to me.

The funny thing was, she really did get through to me, although I didn't know it at the time. Those words stuck with me until I really began to understand what they meant. It's not just some silly expression; it's practically an ethos. Within that overused phrase is self-acceptance, self-reliance and self-confidence.

If you break it down, it goes very well with the idea of choosing to be happy, because it's another way you exercise control over your life. If you don't take shit from anyone, that means you're making the decision to reject negativity and allow only what makes you happy or builds you up to filter through. Positivity rules.

My mom always spoke to me like that, even when I was young, using adult words and in an adult way, and I have to give her credit for that.

I've come to discover I also have some very adult-like conversations with my own children, likely one of the very positive traits I've picked up from her along the way. Occasionally, the language is just as colorful.

In this instance, she was telling me that it was my life and I needed to take a stand when something mattered to me. She was encouraging me to be the passionate, driven person, I would eventually become.

Of course, you can always overdo it. In many instances, that would be my bullheaded way of coping, but in one particular situation in the coming years, I all but forgot those sacred words and paid a very high price for that lapse in judgment. I was about to take a boatload of it!

As I've alluded, my mother and I definitely clashed over the years. There were times I absolutely despised her, and others where I needed nothing more than the feeling of her presence.

She is brash, bold, and proud, and we've both come a long way in how we communicate with each other. Ironically, I credit my husband with showing me how to improve my communication with others, which hugely improved my relationship with my mother.

My parents are two very different people whose differences compliment one another and allow each other to flourish. I believe this is the secret to any long marriage and something I feel within my own.

Though we definitely had some struggles during my teenage years, now we've become closer than ever. Sometimes it just takes a few years (or a few decades!) to adjust to your parents after you become an adult. Even now, as good as things are between us, I'm still aware that our relationship takes work, as do all relationships.

My dad, on the other hand, has always been my hero. As much as my mother and I seemed to just naturally butt heads, my father and I always just got along. He's always been a hard-working guy, which I definitely respect, never asking for anything to be handed to him. He puts in the effort naturally, an ease that extended into our relationship as well. He always enjoyed working out too, so once I became interested in running and weight training, he was very happy for me to tag along with him.

We'd go for runs together or hit the gym, which was a great way to bond. There's something about working up a good sweat that kind of erases all the bullshit. It clears your head, and I was always glad to share that with my dad. On a long run, I remember he'd always smoke me, too.

Some of my fondest memories from childhood are the years I competed in track. Our practices and meets were held after school, mostly while he was still at work, but he'd often take a car he was working on out for a "test drive" and show up for my track meets and surprise me.

It was an awesome thing for him to do. I knew he was busy whenever I invited him to see me compete, and he'd always tell me he would try to be there, but the fact was that he'd almost always find a way to show up for me.

My dad believed in me every single day, and it showed in my performance. Whenever I knew he was out there watching me, it made me run a little bit faster and push a little bit harder.

His pride in me is exactly what I want to show my own kids in whatever they decide to do. I know that even if I had not been a competitive athlete, my dad still would have supported me and been proud of whatever I did.

SEX, DRUGS, AND ROCK AND ROLL

During my freshman year in high school, I had become very depressed. One afternoon before a track meet, I took a handful of over-the-counter pain pills in the girl's locker room. It was not a true suicide attempt, but a cry for help.

I didn't want to die, I just wanted the pain to go away. I was desperate for someone to help me, but I didn't know how to ask for help, because I really didn't know what was wrong with me. In retrospect, I was clearly calling attention to my internal struggles.

The pain I carried for so long of not fitting in, not being the way I envisioned myself, was slowly killing me. When you're a teenager, everything seems bigger than it is, more dramatic, and that is especially true for girls, I think.

Your hormones are raging and your emotions are heightened. Any perceived slight or drama is magnified; everything seems like it's the end of the world.

For healthy kids, those feelings pass. But I was not a healthy kid. I had real inner demons that were driving some very self-destructive behavior. A girl I knew on the team saw what I'd done and ran to get help. Within minutes, *though it felt like an eternity*, one of the football players came running into the girl's locker room.

He scooped me up in his arms and ran to the office like I was a football and the principal was the goal line. I was conscious, but completely panicked since I knew I would be found out, though I do suppose that was kind of the desired result. My cry for help would soon be realized...again.

My mother rushed over to the school from work, while

an ambulance arrived to rush me to the hospital, where I was forced to drink activated charcoal. If you haven't had that experience personally, I will say it's pretty awful and I don't recommend it.

If I thought it was embarrassing for people to know I saw a shrink for body issues, what the fuck was I thinking doing something like that in public? I must have been out of my mind.

Oh, right...

The bottom line is, my ignorant younger self was more calculating than even I realized. I was looking for attention in a way no one ever should. Even thinking about it now, after all these years, makes my skin crawl. To scare the living hell out of my parents like I did was inexcusable.

The worst part was watching my father cry.

Back to the shrink I go, this time on suicide watch and now family counseling added to the mix. My dad, the big tough mechanic, the sweet guy that could talk your ear off about anything, my biggest supporter, my calming force, sat before me and the doctor and wept like a baby.

The thought of losing his little girl was one of the only things I've ever seen this man shed a tear over in my lifetime. I did that to him and I still feel ashamed.

I made my father cry, and somehow that made it all worse.

But it wasn't just him. My mother was deeply affected by my behavior, too. The pain I inflicted upon my parents during that time is something I have suppressed since it happened and something I hope they have forgiven me for.

We have never discussed it since we got through it, which was probably a mistake. Sunlight, as they say, is the best disinfectant. But there is also a time and place for everything, and truth be told, I probably wasn't ready before now.

As I write this, the pain it evokes from deep within is something I have not churned up in over twenty years, and as a result it feels as fresh as when it first happened.

The feeling of reliving many of these situations has brought about anxiety and fear. Fear of judgment is the greatest fear I've ever known and yet somehow, the release of that fear has awakened forgiveness in me I've never allowed myself until now.

I feel horrible for the things I did, not only to myself, but to those that care deeply for me. My parents loved me and I had crushed them. I wholeheartedly believe, that as painful as that time was, I needed to have all of those experiences. Owning my behavior is the only way I can truly move past it.

> *"Like a butterfly stuck in a chrysalis, waiting for the perfect moment, I was waiting for the day I could burst forth and fly away and find my home."*

To accept ourselves, we have to forgive ourselves. That means we accept everything we've ever done and everything we'll ever do. There is no partial self-acceptance. It's all or nothing is this lifetime.

But even the shameful experience of watching my father brought low with grief for his fourteen year-old daughter was not enough to stop my spiraling self-destruction.

Throughout high school, I experimented with nearly every drug offered to me. To this day I don't understand why I was so rebellious or what I was trying to prove.

Most of the kids were into drugs to a certain extent, but

I was always looking to get high and to escape. It was just another way to numb the pain, I guess.

And of course, that filtered down into my sex life.

I've always had a boyfriend. The older guys in high school seemed so much more self-assured than the guys my age, but the truth was that they were mostly just as confused and insecure as everyone else.

That's the big secret of high school: Everybody wants to fit in and nobody thinks they do. Inside, we're all just looking for acceptance from others and not realizing it comes only from ourselves.

Accept yourself, and the world will follow. Easier said than done!

So I hung with my older boyfriend and tuned out the world as much as I could. He was very good to me and we were inseparable.

Eventually, I became as dependent on being in a relationship as I did chasing a high. I shut out friends; I was completely consumed by him and I lost my sense of self.

As a matter of fact, I've never really been alone and never known what it was like to be independent. From the time I was fifteen, I've always been in a relationship. I had the same boyfriend all through high school.

He was good to me and I was terrible to him. It's almost like a setup for what was to come. I had the good guy and took him for granted. I'd soon learn the other side of that coin was not so appealing.

I remember being very envious of my girlfriends who went off to college all alone, without the drag of a relationship. In my mind, they were able to discover their identity much younger than I did.

Looking back, I can see that all of those many lessons were there for me if I was only willing to listen. But not until I was willing did I learn some very tough lessons. I was meant to go through everything I endured to get to where I am today. I eventually realized that the grass is not necessarily greener on the other side, but greenest where you water it.

My dependency on men would eventually prove every bit as dangerous as my dependency on drugs.

A WAY OUT

It's ironic to discover an insatiable hunger to build a strong healthy body out of that same muscle I once diligently worked to starve off my small frame.

How did I get here; how did I turn this corner so sharply? I discovered something so exciting and personally satisfying. I fell in love with building my body instead of breaking it down. Bodybuilding became my world.

How's that for a twist? There I was, born with the perfect build to lift weights or compete in nearly any sport I enjoyed, but I'd been working hard for years to lose all my natural muscle and disappear into the folds of my clothing, all in an attempt to avoid attention.

Shrinking in front of your friends and family is not a very good way to blend in, it would seem. I was actually denying one of my strengths and turning a positive into a negative, which is the opposite of what I should have been doing.

It sounds almost comical now, but that's usually the way it is when we emerge from the fog of self-delusion. I doubt there are very many people walking this earth who have not asked themselves at one point or another the eternal, human question:

WHAT WAS I THINKING?

Whether it's a bad relationship or an addiction or even a job you hate, you can't let yourself become so deluded or complacent that you don't realize how unhappy you are.

If happiness is a choice, then to make that choice requires self-awareness. If you want to fix a problem, you have to first identify it.

It can be very difficult. Trust me, I know. When you're in the middle of that fog, that state of self-delusion, it can be very hard to step outside yourself and see things as they really are.

That was my biggest problem for many years and I was about to find my way out, only to be sucked right back in due to my passionate, yet addictive personality.

You've heard that expression about too much of a good thing being bad for anyone? I could have been the poster child for that because of my passion and drive. When I want something, I go after it with every fiber of my being. Moderation has never been in my vocabulary, but even type A personalities need to practice it once in a while.

During high school, I discovered weight lifting and instantly fell in love. I had always been athletic, even when I was in the clutches of anorexia, and it did me a world of good to focus on my body in a positive way again. It was the opposite of what I'd been doing, and the change in me was immediate.

When you lift weights, you naturally want to see the result of all the hard work you're doing, so simply by closely observing my body and my muscles after lifting, I began to see myself as I actually was.

I could watch the changes almost as they occurred, workout by workout, and it made an enormous difference in my attitude.

It's strange, but by focusing on building my body, I was able to step outside myself and see things as they really were. With anorexia, I was more concerned with the outside world and how other people saw me, which was clouded by my own delusional thinking.

I looked in the mirror and saw a person who was not

really there. I was tearing down my body and my spirit as well, and weight training did the opposite.

After a workout I looked in the mirror and saw progress, and that progress fueled my desire for more. I traded hope for despair. But deep within those moments of focusing on my training, it was like therapy for my sadness and anger. I could let out my aggression on the weights and not those who cared for me the most. I was breaking myself down, forging a stronger, more solid foundation to build on.

I took my power back and it felt damn good!

It all happened because one day the wrestling coach noticed me and suggested I take his weightlifting class.

Weightlifting? I'm trying to starve myself and you want me to bulk up?

But I was in therapy and starting to come out of the fog, and his suggestion caught me at the perfect time. I was intrigued, and when I discovered there was only one other girl in the class, that raised my level of interest exponentially since I liked nothing more than to give the guys a run for their money. I've always felt girls could do anything boys could do, better!

Clearly, I had the very same misconception about weight training as many do. If you lift weights, you will become manly. It doesn't happen that easily, I'm afraid. In training for several national level figure competitions and repeatedly placing in the top five and winning an overall title, I know firsthand how much food, exercise, and sleep it takes to grow muscle. It takes lots of hard work.

You don't accidentally find yourself looking like Arnold Schwarzenegger as a female unless you're doing something "extra" to help it along.

I never had that interest and that was a major factor in my decision to step away from competing after a great run in 2013. When girls in the bikini divisions, who are meant to carry even less muscle mass and definition than the girls in figure, are taking anabolic steroids, where do you go from there? If I had wanted to compete at the pro level, I would have had no chance unless I did the same, and that's when I decided to tap out.

These days, I love my athletic build, but I very much enjoy being feminine. Presenting a certain appearance has always been important to me, but the badass in me loves to push myself harder than anyone else ever could, and I get that fix in the gym.

To this day. I thank Coach Miller for encouraging me to take his class all those years ago. He even tried to get me on the football team, but I think he just wanted to make the local news at that point!

Not only did lifting assist with improving my poor body image, it also helped me as an athlete. I showed up day in and day out. I learned Olympic lifts and proper body mechanics and technique and I couldn't get enough.

I got positive attention for being built the way I was and I liked it. No longer seeing the stares and attention to my athletic body as a negative, I had now come to accept it was a good thing and made the choice to see it as such.

Men's and women's bodies have different natural strengths of course, but as a competitive type, I always like to go up against the best. If I could do one more rep than one of the guys, that was always a sweet victory and good motivation for us both.

More than anything, I was having fun. I couldn't get enough of it. And having fun is half the battle. If you love what you're doing, it doesn't feel like work. And if it doesn't feel like work, your attitude will improve immensely. I looked forward to that class every day and when it was over I wanted more.

I joined a gym and still wanted more, so I hired a personal trainer, and that was the beginning of my interest in fitness competitions and the beginning of my self-acceptance.

I began to accept the way I was built and let go of what I would never be. If you're five feet tall, chances are you'll never play pro basketball, but you may be the perfect size for a jockey.

Or your passion might be in the arts, or you might excel at something no one's ever before attempted or imagined. Loving yourself for your own unique gifts is part of self-acceptance and what I strive to instill in my children.

I tell my kids every day that they are capable of great things, and whether or not they are the same things I can do, I will love and support their choices.

Self-awareness leads to self-acceptance, and that's really the key to happiness. When you accept yourself with all your strengths and weaknesses and understand who you really are, you can make the choice to be happy. I was finally able to do that.

But it didn't last.

Lifting weights outside school and sports kept me out of trouble for a while. One of my first jobs was at a local health club, which was my dream job at that time. It may very well have been, except that was where I met *him*.

My life was about to change in ways I wouldn't soon forget. Just as I was emerging from my fog of self-delusion,

I became involved with a much more dangerous delusion. A delusion of personality. A delusion that someone I should have known was bad for me could be good for me.

A delusion that I could change someone into who I wanted them to be.

I know, this sounds like a cliché, some chick that thought she could change a man. But this was a dangerous man, a man with delusions of his own, a man I should have run away from.

According to the Justice Department's Bureau of Justice and Statistics, *"young women between the ages of 16 and 24 experience the highest rate of intimate partner violence, almost three times the national average."*

I will not name the person who nearly destroyed me. I choose only to call him my *abuser*. There are many reasons for this, not the least of which is my own safety.

And in a sick way, I think he would enjoy the attention.

THE ABUSER

I was 18 and working at my hometown gym, being that I spent much of my time there, anyway. He would come in most weekdays during my shift and he was definitely sizing me up. I was shy and self-conscious around him. He was older and seemingly far out of my league, I recall thinking.

I had just graduated high school and was working part-time at the gym that summer before starting classes at my local community college. I had begun modeling in high school and was represented by several agencies in Ft. Lauderdale and South Beach (SoBe as we locals called it) in my effort to become a fitness model.

I had accepted my body and discovered a very healthy relationship with exercise and food by that point. I was having fun modeling for lots of print and commercial projects along with acting in small roles in film and television.

South Florida had become the backdrop for lots of movies and I was cast in small roles in Wild Things, Holy Man, and Analyze This, as well as several TV series and pilots. Not surprisingly, I was always cast as the girl in a bikini, which worked out just fine now that I was healthy and happy with my fit body.

He was a pilot at a local flight school, very fit and good-looking. Confident in a cocky, almost arrogant way. I've never had a lack of interest from men, but I had been in a relationship with my high school boyfriend until my senior year.

After that relationship ended, I was happy to be single and having fun with friends. On one movie set I was extremely flattered when a well known actor took an interest in me. He sent the director over with a handwritten note, asking to see me. It said something about wanting to "work out together at his hotel."

I nearly died.

Some of the other female talent were envious and no longer seemed to like me, but I had done nothing to initiate it, although I was not unhappy to encourage it, either.

We connected at the Wrap Party (the celebration at the end of filming a movie) and you could say he was awfully handsy for someone dating Cameron Diaz at the time. We danced on the table at Mo's Cantina all night while the other women glared at me. I just smiled and enjoyed every moment of it.

It was certainly fun while it lasted...

Back in the gym, my new friend had become more and more flirtatious with me until one day he came right out and asked for my number. There were plenty of attractive women at my gym, many closer to his age, but he had his eye on me. I can't say I was disappointed. At the time I didn't realize that was his M.O., to find younger, more impressionable women he thought he could manipulate.

The day he asked me out, I was outwardly very cool about it, but very nervous inside. I had developed a huge crush on him, which was obvious and mutual. I think we both knew what was going to happen.

That night, we went on our first date. I remember being quite intrigued by him, probably because he treated me like he could take me or leave me, which was strange because he's the one that came after me.

I'd have never had the nerve to initiate anything with a man eight years older, but it was he who began showing his interest very boldly as the weeks went on.

He had a confidence about him that made me want him all the more. Up to that point, I didn't have to chase after any man, but I was not used to his type. I was young, blonde and fit, and could seemingly take my pick of any single man in the room and I certainly knew it.

This guy, however, made it challenging, which I really liked. I was a born competitor, and if something was hard to get, that made me want it all the more. You could say his stock went up. He was snarky and arrogant, but I was young and didn't see through his facade. He was weak, pretending to be strong, and for a while I bought his act.

I realize now that being referred to as a "fine young thing" while on his arm was not a term of endearment. It was more like I was his possession. It was also the beginning of a degrading, abusive relationship that would waste three years of my life, devastate me mentally and physically, and take nearly another three years to recover from even after it ended.

Shame on me for so many things up to that point in my life, but by far, not understanding the harmful effect this man had on my self-esteem and safety, was the most devastating. I was young and attracted to the "bad boy" and he fit that description to a T.

I fell for him, and I fell hard. But it wasn't love; it was the fascination of an immature girl who had no idea what she really wanted. I look back at that girl now and I want to shake her to her core. I want to warn her about people like this, weak people who prey on the weaknesses of others.

It's all so clear to me now, but why couldn't it have been then? Oh right, I wouldn't have had the opportunity to learn the lesson, though I could've done without this one in particular.

> *"When the student is ready, the teacher will appear."* - Buddhist Proverb

Things were fun at first. Exciting. I was happy that an older, worldly and handsome man had chosen me. I discovered he had quite the sexual appetite and what some might call a strange sexual fetish. He had an addiction to having sex in public places.

I went along with it, sharing for a time, the thrill he got from the risk of being caught. It was like a game to him, and because I wanted to please him, I became eager to participate.

To be honest, I was afraid of losing him.

That should have been my first clue as to the dynamics of our relationship. Anytime you're pressured to do something that makes you uncomfortable, it's a sign that your partner cares more about their own needs than yours.

A relationship should be an equal partnership, but in this case, I was definitely the junior partner. Each of our escapades seemed to be more outrageous than the last. He could get extremely moody and aggressive if I denied him, so I learned quickly to avoid his wrath by becoming something extraordinarily outside my character, submissive.

Our efforts to outdo each previous sexual escapade led us to having sex in outrageous places. Each felt like a notch on his belt, a sex list so long I'm embarrassed to have participated in his twisted game, yet grateful to have never been arrested for public indecency.

There I go, making my parents proud.

He was also extremely jealous and possessive. On many occasions we'd fight if he saw or imagined he saw another man looking at me. It became my fault that I was attractive, and I was called a "slut" or a "whore" for no reason other than his own insecurities.

Even though he had taken a dominant role in our relationship, in time, he could not bury the spirit I had been born with, and our fights were loud, physical, and frightening. No matter how young and naive, I was not about to sit back and say nothing when he attacked me so irrationally. I started fighting back and that was a big mistake.

Sex even became more violent. He'd apologize after becoming aggressive with me for whatever the perceived behavior was that "had made him that way," and then try to have sex. If I didn't let my guard down and appease him, he would become very forceful. Many times I'd submit to him because I thought that was the only way to make the anger and fighting stop. Other times, it would happen regardless.

He'd have his way with me and often the aggressive behavior would start all over again. I know he was an alcoholic and I've always wondered if he was also bipolar.

Clearly, I'm the crazy one to have stayed.

I had become so frail and broken and my mind was so twisted in thinking this was love and how passionate he was to show it in this way. No, that was NOT love, that WAS control.

Please hear me very clearly; someone that loves and respects you does not treat you with ownership, like a trophy or possession. Love does not hurt and sex should never be forceful. I realize now that I was actually raped several times during our relationship when I did clearly say no, but he would not be stopped. Women think that if you are in a relationship with a man, it's not rape.

I myself did not view it that way because we were together, however, the definition of rape is "forcing another to have sexual intercourse against their will."

He raped me.

He probably wasn't used to women challenging him, and his behavior became even more frightening and dangerous over time. It would've served me well to know the future, at this point in time, that I would soon have a loaded gun held to my head. Each time he acted out in rage, he later apologized profusely and promised never to do it again.

But that was after he accused me of "making" him do it.

Again, at that point I should have known things weren't going to get better. I should have left him immediately, but I didn't. This is the difference between the naiveté of youth and the wisdom that comes from experience, and the reason for sharing my story. I can't go back in time and fix my mistakes, but it's my hope to help other women in that position to avoid them or seek help to escape before time is no longer.

More and more, he often did things designed to scare the living hell out of me, but also make me afraid to leave him. He criticized me for everything. No matter what I did, he found fault. He tried to make me believe that no other man would ever want me.

One of the very first times I had ever been up in a plane was with him. As a flight instructor, he had access to the school's planes and took me up one day. I was a bit fearful to begin with, having never flown before.

Without any notice, he killed the engine and flipped us upside down, leaving us barreling through the sky. We were literally free falling back to earth. I thought if I survived, I'd never fly again. Why was he such an asshole? What real purpose did it serve?

Other times we'd fight and he'd kick me out of the car

and leave me on the side of the road far from home. This was long before I had a cell phone. Once, I had to walk to a payphone nearly two miles from where he ditched me. I called my parents and they came to pick me up. I gave them some lame excuse to protect him, though their distaste and disapproval would continually grow along with his aggressive behavior.

He belittled me daily in an effort to break my spirit, hoping I'd never leave him. He wanted to tear down my self-confidence to the point I would become dependent on him.

He almost succeeded.

This psychological mind fuck was a daily occurrence, and yet somehow I hid it from my parents, or at least I thought I did. It was almost like the anorexia, which deluded me into thinking no one would notice. I became withdrawn and couldn't believe I'd allowed this piece of shit to control me.

The fact that he knew of my previous struggle with anorexia made it even more reprehensible. I confided in him and he used it against me. He was a truly disgusting person, a weak-minded predator who made me pay the price for his own insecurities.

As with my eating disorder, I was, in reality, fooling no one except myself. My parents may not have known all the gory details, but they could see that I was desperately unhappy and they could tell he was an asshole. His arrogance masquerading as self-confidence did not fool the people who loved me the most.

Eventually, they begged me to leave him, and that was without knowledge of how abusive things truly were. They hated his egotistical ways without knowing how much worse things were behind closed doors.

With the exception of the time his German Shepherd, much larger than myself, lunged at me and nearly took my hand off. It was the second time he had attacked me. He'd trained the dog to be just as nasty as he was and to take commands only in German.

My hand was a bloody mess of shredded skin wrapped in a kitchen towel. We rushed to the ER. My parents were called and my mother jumped in the car and came barreling into the hospital waiting room not long after we arrived.

She took one look at him and told him to "get the fuck out" and demanded the dog be put down. Knowing he had now attacked me for the second time and that it had also happened to others, she felt grateful my hand was the only casualty that night.

I still bear the faded scars from both attacks on my right hand, another disgusting reminder of my poor choices. Faded too, is the tattoo I got on my right ankle while we were together. I currently undergo painful laser treatments to get rid of it completely.

I could not believe the emotion associated with my first laser treatment. I had put off having it removed because I had always assumed the scar would be worse than the tattoo itself. Learning more about the laser technology now available, I was amazed with the results I'd seen, so I eagerly agreed. It was time to rid myself of this constant memory.

After my first treatment, I removed the protective goggles my doctor had given me, and a stream of tears came rushing down my face. I apologized profusely and with tender tears in her own eyes, she responded that it was quite normal to have a release of emotion with the release of something permanently etched on your body.

A reminder of that awful time of my life, it was far more

emotional than I realized walking into it. But I felt giddy on the way home. It was like I was erasing him from my life. Even after the dog attack, it was not enough to persuade me to leave him.

He defended his violent aggressive dog. I had done nothing to provoke the dog and he was defending THE DOG! But, there was a giant bunch of stupid going on. While he was defending the dog to me, I was defending him to my parents.

I'm ashamed to admit that, but I felt like I was protecting them by doing so. My father was a very level headed guy and it took a lot to set him off, but I knew if he learned what I was dealing with, he'd have beaten the living hell out of my boyfriend and potentially gone to jail.

In my mind, I was saving face for everyone.

In reality, I was prolonging the misery.

Now I can see his type coming from miles away, but back then, I allowed him to slowly entrap me and foster a dependency in me as if he was a drug and I was an addict. I began to drink heavily during this time to deal with the stress of our dysfunctional relationship.

The unexpected emotional ups and downs were like a roller coaster I never thought I'd get off of. Although I was underage, he knew everyone at all of our local hangouts and I guess they thought they were doing him a favor allowing his much younger girlfriend to illegally drink. Risking the loss of their liquor license seems risky, but somehow he'd schmoozed them as he'd done me.

Not long after that, I got a fake ID, so it didn't much matter. The constant physical and verbal abuse was taking its toll, and I began to use alcohol as a coping mechanism for the hell I found myself living in. I became much more aggressive while drinking heavily, and although I felt it was a numbing agent for the pain I was in, it was encouraging even more violent outbursts.

If I could drink until I passed out, that was preferable to another screaming match, though the drinking ultimately brought on more fighting.

Life was like the back of a shampoo bottle, "lather, rinse, repeat" except it was "drink heavily, fight aggressively, come back for more pain and suffering." The more I'd fight back or resist his ways, the harder he'd fight and it was nothing short of Mr. and Mrs. Smith minus the special effects.

In short, I was a fucking mess.

Everyone around me could see he was no good, everyone but me. Deep down, I knew this wasn't what I deserved, but I had been succumbing to this behavior for so long that it had become my new normal.

I was afraid to be with him and yet afraid to let him go. Because of his mind games, I actually began to believe that being controlled in this manner was to be loved.

In some sick, twisted way, I felt wanted. So I stayed with him far too long.

As terrible as this sounds, it is not unusual. **According to the World Health Organization,** *1 in 4 women will be victims of severe violence at the hands of her husband or boyfriend. In the United States, a woman is beaten every nine seconds.*

I was one of them.

Leaving that horrific relationship was one of the hardest things I've ever done, until one day I gained an amazing strength I had never known before.

> *"I will protect myself from those who do not have my best interests at heart." – TLG*

MY REBIRTH

It began with a work out.

A long, hard, sweaty workout to drive the demons back down into my subconscious where I continually tried to keep them at bay, which of course only made them stronger and more eager to rise to the surface. I took my aggressions out on my body. I ran. Far and fast. The sweat was a release of the poison I carried inside.

I lifted weights until I could no longer lift my arms. I'd train to the point of failure. I sought the aftermath of sore, tired muscles. I would occasionally shed tears during my runs. Tiny tears I created within to release my anger. I ran without music during much of that time. It cleared my mind.

I often envisioned leaving and how I would do it. My thoughts then returned to him coming after me and never allowing that to happen. I was fearful, I was hurt, but more than anything, I was beginning to become extremely angry toward everything in my life.

The deeper you bury your problems, the more troublesome they become. Ignoring what's wrong doesn't make it go away, it only makes it worse. Especially when what's wrong is you.

I will grant you that my abuser was a big part of my problem at the time, but he wasn't the cause. He was a symptom.

He was nothing more than an opportunistic predator who came along at the perfect time to take advantage of my youthful demons, the inner fears that had driven me to addiction and self-destructive behavior.

Why did I gravitate to bad boys? Why did I put up with

someone who was abusive? Why didn't I just leave him?

Too many whys and not nearly enough wisdom.

I wasn't that same shy little girl without understanding of the adult world, not knowing how to respond to a grown man admiring my muscular body. I was now a grown woman, a strong woman, and yet I seemed helpless to break free of the monster that slept beside me.

To a certain extent, it still baffles me today.

If it sounds confusing to you, imagine what went through my head each night I woke and spent another day with him. I was filled with shame and anger at both him and myself for remaining in my situation, even as I was the picture of health and vibrancy on the outside.

Everything should have been wonderful. I had just returned from a week in the Caribbean where I'd shot several episodes of an Aaron Spelling television show on a cruise ship, and at that point, I'd finally been able to turn my body issues into a positive force through weight training. Yet I was still desperately unhappy.

Never judge a book by its cover. The happy person you see at social gatherings or even on social media, may not be the happy, confident person they appear to be.

I certainly wasn't.

I was angry with myself for a long time for staying in a dangerous situation with an abusive partner, but just as I learned not to judge others so harshly, I have learned to extend myself the very same courtesy.

One of the most powerful lessons I learned during that difficult time was simply to be good to myself, to truly understand that I was deserving of happiness, as we all are. And of course, that was also something that helped me escape his tight grip.

That, and a fantastic guy who saw something in me I didn't yet see in myself, and who refused to take "no" for an answer when I turned him down.

Ten times.

As persistent as he was, it also didn't hurt that he was very handsome.

But on the day I met the love of my life, I was still living in my nightmare.

And that's how it was, that on one of the best days of my life, I still spent the night with a monster.

I was near the end of my workout when he walked in, and when I say walked in, that does not begin to describe it.

My husband is one of those people who enters a room and commands it. There's just something about him that demands attention, whether he's actively seeking it or not.

He has an inner strength and confidence that comes through in everything he does, and on that day, before he said a single word, I knew he was something special.

But I was 'involved.'

For three long, miserable years, I'd been with a jealous, controlling, manipulative man. That type of relationship can be as difficult to get out of as it is to continue, and that's how it was for me.

I was very fortunate though; in that the man I would marry was everything my abuser was not. Strong, kind, compassionate, driven to succeed, and most importantly, capable of true love.

None of which I knew when the big, handsome man I'd

noticed in the mirror eyeing me out of the corner of his eye finally walked over to say hello as I was finishing my last set of squats.

Squats are miserable and extremely effective, so just watching him in the mirror, out of the corner of my eye, had gotten me through the last several reps.

"Impressive," he said, smiling.

I was thinking the same thing, but all I managed to say was, "Thanks."

But I smiled back.

He introduced himself and we chatted about the gym a bit. He was there on business and I wasn't sure for how long, but I could tell he was interested and he wasn't trying to hide it one bit.

I love the gym, but I go there to put in work. Not everyone does, however. As a woman, you discover this pretty quickly.

"I'd love to pick your brain sometime," he said.

"Excuse me?" I wasn't sure I'd heard correctly.

"I said I'd love to talk to you more and I'd like you to show me around since I'm new here and don't really know anyone."

I smiled. He seemed like a really nice guy, polite and respectful, as I said, everything my current partner was not. But I wasn't born yesterday. I could tell he liked me, and not only for my "brains."

He seemed to sense my amusement, and he smiled boyishly, which I found quite charming. "Okay, I would also like to get to know you better," he said. Just as I had suspected.

Wow, He really is the opposite of what I've been dealing with!

Right out of the gates, feeling his vibe, I blurted out, "I have a boyfriend." I couldn't believe those words came out of my mouth.

He must have seen something in my eyes as I spoke those words, because he looked at me very intently, straight in the eyes as if he could see the turmoil. If the eyes are truly the windows of the soul, he'd seen into mine.

It felt like forever until he spoke, although it was probably just an instant, but that look in his eyes told me that he wasn't about to give up on me, and he sparked a tiny flame of hope in my heart that would grow to become a passionate bonfire that continues to this day. I am still giddy about this boy of mine, even more than 16 years later.

"I'll see you around in that case" he said, and took my hand in both of his. There was something warm and strong and reassuring about the way he touched me. Caring but not intrusive, strong but not confining.

This time it was me who blushed. "I'm sure you will."

And we did. But it took a while for things to develop.

I felt lighter than air on the way home. It probably looked like the most casual of encounters from across the room, and the truth was, it was just a little minor flirting. But there was something about the man that wasn't casual.

He knew what he wanted in life and he went for whatever it was. That was so obvious he might as well have it tattooed across his forehead.

He was a man with a plan and any woman who partnered with him would be a lucky woman, indeed, because he knew how to treat a woman.

I spent that night with my boyfriend at his place, and it was one of the worst. We had a terrible fight. I think I had seen a tiny bit of what I'd been missing, and the anger at my abuser and myself came out in full force.

I'm not sure there was any coincidence, rather a full on message hitting me harder than he ever had. I believe, with all of my being, that was no accident.

He did not like it when I gave him "attitude." He felt threatened by my intellect and opinions, because it called attention to what he lacked. Things got physical, and I fought back. It was an ugly scene.

He kept a loaded gun on the headboard of the bed, and this would be the night he pointed it *at my head*. I actually felt my entire body go completely limp as I peered down the barrel. I don't recall what I said to calm him down, but as I finally relented, he began to come out of his rage. He apologized profusely, cried and begged for forgiveness. I was in complete shock and more numb in that moment than in any alcohol induced stupor I'd experienced.

That night, I slept with one eye open, but when I dreamed, I dreamed about John.

Around that time, I was also doing more acting and modeling. I enjoyed it and it came naturally to me, but that kind of attention really bothered him and it made our relationship all the more miserable.

I believe he sensed that the more successful I became, the more jobs I booked, the more likely he was to lose me. I was like some exotic bird in a cage, with beautiful feathers he wanted to possess as long as no one else ever heard my song. I was finally beginning to understand the true meaning behind his efforts to control me.

A person with a healthy ego wants their partner to

succeed and is flattered that others see that person as desirable. I am always thrilled to see others succeed, but he couldn't handle it if I got any attention at all. He would fly into a rage if another man so much as glanced at me, which was a huge problem, because it definitely happened.

When we went out, if people looked at me, whether men or women, he absolutely hated it. None of it was worth fighting about, but it became our routine and alcohol further heightened the drama.

He seemed to invent things to complain about. I became convinced he was neurotic, as I could barely speak to my own friends by this point, male or female. Control freak at its finest.

So you can only imagine the hell I endured after appearing on a television show or film set and met lots of attractive people with similar interests.

I landed some small roles and even worked as a stunt double during that time, which I found to be far more thrilling, actually. It filled my need for adrenaline. It was a very exciting time in my life, a time I was learning more about who I was and who I wanted to be.

I was having a blast and my family couldn't have been more supportive. I was meeting lots of great people and most of them were highly optimistic and positive in nature, something I had withdrawn from in my own world.

But he never supported any of that. He was completely against anything that made me happy and would get very angry when I went on auditions. It was a fun hobby for me, an outlet for my boundless energy, but he made me feel terrible about it and everything else I had an interest in.

Looking back, the hypocrisy is unreal. The very things that attracted him to me in the first place, were completely off limits to any other human being.

I began to temper my enthusiasm simply to avoid a fight, which is ridiculous. Who hides their happiness to please a miserable person? I did. That led to me harboring extreme resentment towards his lack of support or happiness for my achievements. All I received was jealousy.

That was my crazy life.

But through it all, I kept running into John at the gym, a gentleman in every sense of the word, and he kept asking me out. My parents worked out there as well and he had introduced himself to them.

My mother took a real liking to him and continued to encourage me to date him, as she knew he had a definite interest in me. He'd been serious about wanting to go on a date and I had been serious in denying him, but the truth was that he wanted me, and I wanted him, too.

I was on a collision course in my current relationship and all of the addictions and destructive behavior that had controlled me to that point in my life.

Would I be able to escape them?

Every time he asked me out, I came closer to saying yes. I was incredibly curious as to how a man like that would treat a woman on a date, and in life.

And yes, in bed.

I'm a passionate woman, and I had begun fantasizing about him, wondering what it would be like to be with him. He was a bit closer in age, only five years older, but there was this special energy around him.

But I was scared. Fearful. My abuser was a joke, but he wasn't funny at all. I was finally at the end of my rope, yet I truly believed he might kill me if he couldn't have me. I was miserable with him and scared to leave him, until I finally decided I owed it to myself to see how a good man would treat me.

So, the eleventh time John Gaston asked me out, I finally said yes.

The look on his face was priceless. He was like the dog that finally caught his tail and is momentarily so shocked he doesn't know how to react. I reached over and put a finger under his chin to close his mouth, and he flashed me that million-dollar smile and quickly recovered.

The night of our first date is a memory I will never forget. I never let him know that I was still in a relationship, but I knew it was ending eminently and I needed to see what it could be like with someone else.

I could tell he liked me, but I made it very clear I would not be getting serious with anyone, after the long hellish relationship I had been in. He understood and wanted to spend time with me no matter how that happened. I can't say I didn't feel the same, I couldn't get enough of him.

John was kind and gentle. Strong and unthreatened by those around him. At one point, I noticed the waiter glancing at my cleavage, one of those tiny, I-just-couldn't-help-myself-peeks, and for an instant I was terrified.

A cold chill ran up my spine instinctually, a result of many public fights I'd endured with my abuser, until I lifted my eyes to his across the table and he burst out laughing.

I joined him in roaring laughter, and at that moment, I knew I was looking at someone I could be with. It was such a tiny thing, but it meant the world to me. It meant that he was secure enough within himself, to be with me.

And he was so interesting! It was amazing to just sit there and listen to his plans to build an empire. I must have been starved for real, adult conversation, because the time just flew by.

He was so motivated to succeed, but it was a healthy motivation, the kind of motivation I had found in myself when I discovered fitness. He was interested in me and my goals and aspirations, something I was not accustomed to during that time.

He told me everything I needed to hear. Right then I knew without a doubt, that there was so much more in the world waiting for me. He was the example to myself to make the change I had been so reluctant to make.

Regardless of what became of my relationship with John, he was the new bar by which all other men would now be measured. And for most of the men out there, that truly sucks for them! They don't make them like John anymore.

When we parted, he planted a single kiss on my lips, a kiss we both wanted to last much longer, and whispered, "I want to see you again soon."

"You will," I promised, to myself as much as to him.

That night, I ended the relationship with my abuser.

All hell broke loose.

Whatever you've seen in the movies or experienced in real life from a stalker commenced. Threatening calls, unexpected visits to my job and home, intimidation of all kinds. Everything he could think of to make me come back to him, he did. He was relentless.

It's incredibly stupid, when you think about it. You want someone back so you treat her like garbage, expecting that to fix things. You cry, you beg, you threaten and intimidate.

And very often, it works.

According to the National Coalition Against Domestic Violence, *85% of women return to abusive relationships.*

I was determined not to be one of them.

I looked into getting a restraining order, something my employer at the time had encouraged when my abuser began to appear at my job. The threats continued regardless and then he told me he was going to kill himself. At that point, I had no choice but to call his family and ask for their help. He was a grown man, then twenty-eight years old, but I had to call his mother; I had to take him seriously.

I was in hiding, and it was a very scary time. I feared he would pull the trigger the next time he raised one of his guns to me or God forbid, someone I loved.

I was happily dating my future husband and my abuser seemed so small in comparison. I had moved on and he was still living in some fantasy world in which he could exercise control over me. By then he was a distant speck on the horizon of my past, a place I could barely believe I'd ever visited.

In time, all of his bullshit subsided, but not until I communicated his suicidal threats to his family. I considered his threats the last effort of a desperate man trying to guilt me into staying, but I was far stronger this time.

Even after all of that, for a time, I lived in constant fear that he would reappear in my life. I had moved out of my parent's house and in with John, so he no longer knew where to find me. It's been awhile since I've looked over my shoulder as I did back then, but years went by before I finally felt he was no longer a threat to me, or the people I love.

It took time to get my confidence back after being

treated so poorly for so long. I spent three years of my life succumbing to the verbal and physical breakdown of my self-confidence and self-esteem.

The mental and physical violence he unleashed on me, was due to his own insecurities. I realize now it took many more years for me to dig back out of that darkness, even after I was finally rid of him.

> *"I forgive those who have harmed me in my past and peacefully detach from them."*

I've come to realize that forgiveness is not something I've given to the abusive man of my past, it is a gift I give myself for the pain I have harbored and suppressed for so many years. The guilt I've carried for allowing this type of treatment. I have finally released myself.

I am sickened that I would ever stay with someone so horrible, but in the midst of being beaten down like that, body and soul, your perspective becomes skewed. Only when you've been in a situation like this can you fully understand why a person stays, or why they go back.

Never judge a book by its cover. Never question another's pain.

With some time passing to sow my wild oats and learn to be me outside of a relationship, as I had never really done, I knew John was the one. We dated for a few months, and he didn't pressure me to make it anything more than that. He knew what I'd gone through before, and he gave me my space.

But I always came back to John. As I said, he was the bar against which all others were measured, and everyone else fell short.

Once I could finally handle being in a committed

relationship, he asked me to marry him. I was just twenty-one and had never been given the value I deserved, until John came into my world. I knew I'd never find someone like him again during my lifetime.

Looking back, it's clear to me that John saved my life. He showed me the importance of protecting myself from those who do not have my best interests at heart, and enabled me to become the best person I could possibly be. To this very day, he still does that for me and our three beautiful children.

My husband, my partner, my best friend.

I can't imagine where I'd be today if I hadn't crossed paths with him that day in the gym, at the end of an intense, emotional workout. I was in the right place at exactly the right time, and that has made all the difference in the path my life has taken.

After many years of marriage, our passion still burns intensely for one another. How tragic it would have been not to have taken that leap of faith so many years earlier.

In my heart, he'll forever be my saving grace.

BREAKING POINT

Even after finding my soul-mate, I still had work to do in our relationship. My learned behavior was difficult to reverse for many years. I harbored such anger and resentment towards my abuser, that it affected me deeply for a very long time. For a long while, releasing it on those closest to me was my easiest mechanism by which to communicate.

I had a difficult time admitting when I was upset or hurt. I'd built an emotional wall for protection and it still existed many years later, a remnant of how much damage had been done.

This made for a very difficult first year of marriage, needless to say. Something had to change if we were going to keep it together.

And I knew it was on me, not the man who saved me and had shown me a better way. He was fighting for me every single day and I was pushing him further and further away.

Married at 21, my first child at 24 and the next at 25, I had entered an adult world I wasn't prepared for. I had never been away from home, yet at 21, I was newly married and living more than 2000 miles from the comfort of my family and friends.

To make things worse, my new husband was working sixteen hours a day, traveling all over the country and grinding hard for a dream no one else could see.

It's sad to think you can have the world and still somehow lack inner peace, but that had become my life. I was lonely, resentful and felt my own worth diminish as he worked diligently to achieve his dream of being retired in his early 30's, which ultimately would become our reality.

But I couldn't see it. I continued to do the things that made me happy, but inside I had never felt more alone. I wondered what was wrong with me. I had become needy, and that neediness affected our marriage.

Looking back on that time, I'm so grateful to have made it through that first year of our marriage. There were times I didn't know if I would. Ultimately, I needed something to focus on rather than just my husband's absence. I was living in his shadow, and that's not where I wanted to be.

My children were a source of great value for me and helped me cope with things, until I hit a breaking point I could have never seen coming.

I realize now that I grew up within our marriage. I was young and it was quite challenging early on because I was coming out of such a horrendous relationship and jumped right back into this one.

There was no getting around the fact that I was flawed. I didn't see it for myself at the time, but I was hot tempered, easily flustered, and out of control. I anchored myself with fitness, which allowed me an outlet away from home and family, but I had also started a new life thousands of miles away from everything I had ever known.

I was, ironically, still very much like that little girl in the hardware store all those years ago, after all. Confused, frightened, and more than a little lost.

My only hope was to learn how to express myself in more productive ways. Without the ability to do so, there were many wild fights and sleepless nights within my new marriage.

How could I go from an abusive partner to a wonderful husband and still find myself unhappy? What could I do to fix things?

As you know by now, I'm a doer. I've never been a passive person, and so I attacked the problem head on.

I became obsessed with being the perfect wife and mother, but you can imagine the results when anyone sets the bar that high. No one can possibly live up to perfection, and I was no exception.

What happened next was a complete shock to my system.

Depression, anxiety, panic attacks, and ultimately, a breakdown.

Many close to me were unaware of my inner turmoil during this time, likely a result of my jaded past, but it was certainly evident within our home. My unhappiness and resentment forced us further apart until we were more like roommates than man and wife.

I desperately wanted his time and attention, but it was as though he could no longer see me. I knew he loved me, but he was working so hard to build his business that he lost himself in it.

I tried hard to be supportive; he was trying to give me the life of my dreams. I just couldn't get past my dependency on him. I had never felt that way until now, living on the other side of the country with no family and very few friends. I felt so alone.

I began to shut down. I had regressed. I felt guilty to have brought children into the world that I didn't feel strong enough to care for in the way they deserved. I sunk deeper and deeper into depression.

It was as if a small piece of my soul had gone missing. I was raising two daughters under the age of 4, 16 months apart in age, with very little help. I was beginning to feel like a single mom. My interests and hobbies were completely irrelevant, as if I had ceased to exist outside the role of "mommy."

My days were planned around naptime, lunchtime, bath time, story time, and bedtime. I tried to keep it together and focus on my beautiful daughters, but there was always the nagging feeling in the back of my mind that I was somehow lost, incomplete. Not a real person any longer, but a shadow of my former self.

And then it happened. I broke down completely and felt helpless to prevent it. Life was not something I had control over anymore, but something that happened to me.

Something had to change.

On the outside I seemed to have it all, but on the inside, I was lost. My identity was gone. Disappeared. I had placed so much value on my looks, that becoming a "mom" and not feeling like the attractive woman I once was, tore me up inside.

I finally understood my feelings the day my husband overheard me on the phone speaking to a web designer. In that moment, what I said broke his heart.

I was trying to re-establish myself in the fitness world, since popping out two kids back to back, and had been working incredibly hard to that end.

I'd gotten myself back into great shape, better than ever, and I was ready to feel like the woman I was before I became a mom. I was ready to have some time for myself to get back to doing what made me tick.

What happened next crushed my husband as he walked in from work and overheard me on the phone with her. She had asked me what I stood for, who my target audience was and what my greatest message was. "I don't just want to be a mom," I said. I'm so much more than just a mom."

Looking back, I can see why those words hurt him so badly. There is no such thing as 'just' a mom. Even recalling that moment and those words now, makes me cringe.

Believe me, I know that being a mother is truly the hardest and most important job I will ever have in this world and one I've come to appreciate far more, now that I feel like myself again.

That said, when John heard those words come out of me, he was devastated. He thought he'd made me the happiest girl in the world, giving me the opportunity to raise our children and stay home with them, but I wasn't. I was unhappy, and that made him unhappy, too.

I couldn't help it, though. I felt a complete loss of my own identity and I had these terrible feelings, feelings that tore me up inside. What happened next was a major turning point in my life.

A terribly difficult turning point.

We had it out. Everything on the table. All our hopes and dreams and fears and insecurities laid bare. It was raw and uncertain and necessary. This was the beginning of me learning to put words to my feelings.

For so long I had felt I no longer had a voice or a purpose beyond being a mother. I felt suppressed in who I had become. I didn't identify it early on, however, and had I communicated those feelings to my husband, he would have fully supported me and helped me through the rough patch.

Things would not have been so bad.

During this time, we fought and struggled and I pushed him away. I feel terrible to have gotten to the point that

I did before acknowledging those feelings, but through the process, we gained such strength in our marriage and developed an even stronger bond. I never wanted to make him feel that he and my beautiful girls weren't enough, but the need for me to feel like I was enough had diminished.

We were fighting, but we were fighting for our marriage, for our family, for our lives. To my husband's credit, he stuck with me. He did not run from the crazy person I had become for the same reason he sought me out in the gym years before.

He saw something in me that I did not yet recognize myself.

There are many things I've learned from my amazing husband over the past 16 years, but the most important thing has been how to communicate. No marriage is perfect and there will always be conflict from time to time, but John taught me how to fight fair.

I cannot emphasize how important that is in a marriage.

I've grown up in my marriage, and I'm grateful for each day I fought to keep it together and for John's patience and willingness to work with me through those challenges.

With his help, a fair bit of counseling, and lots of personal development, I learned how to communicate without hurting others. It's hard to admit your mistakes sometimes, but doing so has set me free.

I have finally escaped the darkness of my past and I no longer live my life in fear. I am in complete control of my happiness, a place I struggled to reach with lots of stumbling along the way.

"Anger will no longer consume me." TLG

It took a while, because my entire life had led me to

where I was. There was a lot to undo, I guess you could say. The behaviors we witness as children are carried into adulthood.

Being treated so disrespectfully for so long by an abusive man had a lasting effect. Placing so much value on my looks, added to the mess I had become. I had sought the wrong kind of attention for so long, it was a hard habit to break.

My breakdown led me to understand just how twisted my own perspective had become. I began to realize how important the things we say to our children are, as well as the tone in which we say them.

I even began to examine the photos I had taken before my children were born. Some of the images I shot long ago were not something I'd want my children to see, and I'm grateful much of that was prior to the digital era. I wanted to represent myself in a far classier way; I didn't need the wrong type of attention, I was already giving that to myself.

The point is that I was learning from my own mistakes and using that knowledge to become a better person, a better wife, and a better mother. I was getting to know who I was, which is not an easy thing to do sometimes.

We are all a product of layer upon layer of experiences, both good and bad. When you're able to strip it all away and understand where you came from, it can help you figure out where you're going.

By the same token, if you discover what makes you tick and you're not fulfilling it, unhappiness will grow from that seed and spread toxicity within until it takes over your life and leaves no way to hide behind it.

That was me. I had shut down and become flat out miserable. My marriage was suffering and we had grown apart. Not only because he was not home very much, but because I never communicated those feelings. I let my unhappiness fester and it drove me away from him, which made me even more resentful.

I had the world at my fingertips and felt like the unhappiest person in it.

Why could I not see how great things were? What was happening to me? I wanted to be the mother my girls needed and the wife my husband married, but the light behind my eyes had faded.

After lots of fighting, it was clear the love was never lost and could in fact become stronger if we wanted to work for it. He acknowledged his absence and the role that had in my feelings at the time.

I believe that because he took accountability and owned a piece of that breakage, it opened our eyes to the value we see in one another to this day.

It was no longer about placing blame and finger-pointing; it was about giving ourselves back to each other wholly and releasing past hurts, resentment, and anger. I had to let down the walls I had built around myself.

I would get so angry because I couldn't communicate my frustrations, but I eventually learned to do so. It takes two people to want to fix something to make it work, and you've never seen two people so passionately in love with each other, fighting so hard for one another.

We discovered a strength within our relationship we never had before. Our eyes and our hearts became more open and forgiving. We are now stronger than ever, and though it was an extremely hurtful time for the both of us, we have both acknowledged its value.

From our darkest hours come our greatest revelations. And so it was for me. You have to be open and willing to hear the lesson being taught if you are to grow from it, and I was. With the love and support from John, I was able to emerge from the darkness to become the person I was meant to be.

First, I had to realize that my husband was completely supportive and it was no fault of his own this had happened. As a type A personality, I had done this to myself. When I finally realized what was making me so unhappy in my life, I made a change.

"My happiness is my choice"

During my darkest moments I pulled myself up, and told myself I could either continue to wallow in self-pity or get up and take a stand for my marriage. I had awakened my inner fighter from the depths of depression, and after a good hard fight, I had regained a positive perspective on my world.

John fought for me from day one and I would fight for us from that moment forward, harder than I ever had.

For my daughters' benefit, I had to finally come to terms with the origins of my anorexia and the lingering effects of an unhealthy obsession with body image.

I decided I wanted to promote fitness and a healthy lifestyle and be a role model for my girls without passing on any of the negative aspects from my earlier years. I could fill that void in my life again by doing what I love and still be a good mother to my girls.

Society can damage us. Images on television, magazines, everywhere you look. When you place your primary value on something so fleeting as appearance, you are setting yourself up for failure.

I recall as a young girl that even my own mother fed

into this. She was constantly on a diet, expressing her dissatisfaction for her body and her weight. I had heard her repeatedly say she felt fat.

I watched all of this, and likely learned some of my own behaviors this way. I decided I would aim to never use words like that about my body in front of my young, impressionable girls.

I have seen what a negative effect and awareness it can bring about and I was fearful for my own daughters to ever share the struggles I've had.

Being praised for your looks since childhood can have a profound effect on a person, especially since looks will undoubtedly fade. It can really screw with your sense of value in this world.

Hearing that if you were abducted or murdered, it would be all over the news "because you're pretty," is kind of a whacked out thing to say to a kid, as I look back.

I love my mother. We had some difficult years, but we made it through. Our relationship has grown and matured just as we have.

I'm cautious about how I speak to my girls when it comes to weight and body image. Believe me, I'm not unaware of what having a mother in this industry can do to a daughter, and because of that, we talk openly about it. I realize seeing their mother on the cover of fitness magazines may carry a heavy responsibility for my approval, or a certain expectation, but it does not.

I want them to feel confident in their own skin and comfortable with themselves and their own special gifts. I tell them often. I made the decision to protect them constantly from what I did to myself at their age.

They know I want them to be happy, healthy, and to believe in their dreams. I know because of that, we have some powerhouse children. I only hope my example serves to inspire or motivate them in some small way.

My message to my daughters has always been: strive for happiness in any shape or size it comes in, because healthy looks different on everyone. Find happiness within yourself for your unique strengths, because that is a gift no one else can give you.

Take charge of your happiness, and never allow it to be dictated by someone else. Love yourself. Never allow another to break your spirit, because that is not love.

Most importantly, love does not hurt. Don't wait until it's too late to get out. I'm lucky I removed myself from what could've been a completely different storyline. If you can't get out, or don't know where to start, ask for help. There are many ways to reach out, whether to a family member or friend, or even the:

National Domestic Violence Hotline
1-800-799-SAFE (7233)
1-800-787-3224

IN CONCLUSION

It's safe to say my story is no fairy tale, but I've built a wonderful life brick by brick over many years and you can do the same with willingness and desire.

My value will never be established by another human being again. I will never accept being treated how I once was, because I'm lucky to have made it out alive.

I remember wondering how a woman could ever stay with a man that abuses her, until I lived that exact scenario, and I stayed. It's shameful, but now I have a complete understanding of what it can do to your mind.

My past has made me the strong woman I am today, and I live without regret. I give myself to others in an effort to help raise them up, because I've discovered that's what makes me happiest.

If you are stuck in an abusive relationship, I understand. There once was a time I needed the courage to escape such a horrible situation. I understand the fear. I want to hold your hand and tell you it's going to be okay.

You may have to hit rock bottom before you get angry enough to fight back, but that day will come. Getting to the precipice of losing everything was my eye opener.

Never judge another's pain unless you've walked a mile in their shoes.

I understand this firsthand, because I was very good at hiding my pain. I displayed a completely different personality in order to hide what I was feeling inside.

I may have come off as uncaring on the exterior, but on the inside, I was deeply hurting. I struggled with communication, something that comes far easier to me now, but something that took a long time to learn how to do properly.

Learn to be a truth teller, to yourself as well as others.

Tell yourself each day, "I am strong, I am beautiful, I am powerful." Listen to those words and believe them, because you are. We all are beautiful in our own way, and we all have our own special gifts. You must fully invest in those words each time you say them.

Do not take them for granted, because they hold tremendous power. The power is in you and your belief that the words are true.

We become what we believe.

Believe in your inner badass!

GIVING BACK

Some of my greatest joy comes from helping others. I'm most contented when I find ways to give back and do something for someone else. Whether it's someone I know or within my community.

For me, to *do* good is to *feel* good.

In joining forces with a local charity here in Phoenix (the Johnjay and Rich Care for Kids Foundation), I'm part of something that gives me fulfillment, while also benefiting the lives of children in the foster care system.

Currently, the number of children in foster care in Arizona, is well over 20,000. This is a horrific, silent epidemic. Far too many of these children go into the system, age out, and then go on to become something other than their best self as adults.

According to the National Center for Health Research, *girls in foster care are twice as likely to get pregnant by the age of nineteen as girls outside the system, and since the United States has one of the highest teen pregnancy rates in the industrialized world, guidance for these young women is crucial.*

Things are just as bleak for boys. Foster kids of either sex who age out of the system, are more likely to be homeless, incarcerated or jobless as they enter adulthood.

I can't help but think, that with the proper guidance and mentorship, some of these kids would have a chance to be so much more.

The very thought that some of these boys will grow up to be aggressive, because of a lack of guidance during their youth, is very frightening to me. The possibility of such aggression being taken out on a woman really resonates with me, which is why I want to be involved in finding solutions. If even one child at a time, there are many ways we can help a child in foster care.

    If you feel as strongly as I do about the value of mentorship, I urge you to find ways to volunteer your time or resources within your community. There are so many ways to help, aside from being a foster parent. Simply spending time to visit with a child that has no family, can make a huge impact within their life. Many just want to be heard, valued and appreciated, when they believe no one cares about them.

WHAT CAN YOU DO?

If you find yourself feeling down, depressed, or unfulfilled, put your ego aside and ask for help. Being able to communicate my feelings with my husband, who is my number one supporter, was the first step in my own self-discovery.

If you can't find the words to ask for help, how can you expect the support of others? All he knew was that I was angry and resentful. I couldn't say or do anything to show him what was going on inside.

I very nearly destroyed my marriage to get the understanding I desperately needed. Don't make the same mistake I did. Find a way to communicate with your loved ones before things get to that point.

Love yourself, and communicate with those who love you.

Meeting your own needs is crucial in becoming genuinely fulfilled. Determine what makes you happy. Without clearly identifying your passions and making time for them, it can be no one else's fault but your own. We all must look inside ourselves to determine what we can do to be better contributors to our situation.

Playing the blame game won't get you anywhere.

And no, it is not selfish to take time out for you! Think about the Golden Rule, and apply it to yourself as well as others. Treat yourself the way you want others to treat you.

Show respect to others and to yourself. If you are proud, confident, and secure in who you are and in your unique gifts, the world will see you that way too.

Working out, eating right, and feeling good about yourself is not only a gift to you, it is a gift to those around you.

When you are fulfilled, you can give even more to others.

THE FIRST STEP

Through much soul searching, I discovered that in order to maintain my happiness, I needed to do things that made Tiffany happy. Sounds simple, but it's not.

When you're a mother, it's easy to define yourself as only that, but as women, we can be whatever we want.

It's not okay to always put yourself last. Your value should be of utmost importance to you if you're going to be worth a damn to anyone else you care for.

Why are we shaming ourselves as wives and mothers for having our own desires, dreams and passions?

So many of us have what I refer to as "mommy guilt" when what we should be doing is showing our children how to juggle all of the many things that are important to us.

Why should we deny ourselves something, simply because society dictates what a wife and mom should be? I say to hell with that! Whether you choose to stay at home and raise your children or go back to work, it's nobody's business but your own.

I'm supposed to completely fade into the background of my own life to be considered a "good mom?"

That's not exactly my style! You must do the things you once did to continue to be fulfilled. No guilt, no explanation, no shame. Being your authentic self is something every woman is entitled to.

With the support of my husband and the love of my three children, I was able to find that balance in my life that allowed me to flourish, and you can do the same.

Choose your happy and find your inner badass. She lives

inside all of us and she should "never take shit from anyone!" as mom would say.

BEING TRUE TO YOURSELF

What should a mother be? In my mind, I struggled with some false idea I needed to live up to, but to whom was I accountable?

I realize now, that happy children are a result of being loved, cared for and encouraged. The goal is to provide that for our children, while maintaining our own true self in the process.

I needed to be the feisty, funny, fearless woman I once was. I was determined to get that back or die trying.

> *"I will chase my dreams with passion and fury, for tomorrow is never promised."* TLG

FINDING BALANCE

We all want to be great mothers and do what's best for our children, but at what cost? Are we really willing to lose ourselves within the role? I still want my husband to feel like my king and we plan weekly date nights when possible.

I need my children to feel listened to, loved and appreciated, but I also need those things for myself.

The discovery that I really could do and be all of those things to all of those important people in my life, as well as fulfilling the goals and desires I had set before myself, was the greatest gift I've ever known.

The beauty in taking control of my life and getting back to doing the things that made me excited, is that everyone around me benefited from it.

My husband had his happy, vivacious wife back and my children had a mom that was fulfilled and eager to give back to them. I discovered that once I was fulfilled, I was eager to give to others. I learned that I couldn't just go around filling everyone else's hearts and not my own.

I had to step up, take control, and be my authentic self. Only then was I worth a damn to others.

If you've ever flown, you've heard the flight attendant say that in the event of an emergency; you must place the oxygen mask on yourself before you help those around you. That's what I mean.

Give yourself room to breathe, so you can help others find their way.

Putting your children first doesn't have to mean you are always last. One of the most important things your children can witness is your own happiness. Happiness is something you exude, the same as frustration, depression, or anger. If you don't think your children are onto you, you're in denial. And while it may not be everyone's mentality to put their marriage ahead of their children from time to time, it is now mine.

In order to maintain a happy marriage, we must be a tight unit. We're a team and the greatest thing our children can witness is the love and affection we share.

We parent better when we're on the same page and if that means making a weekly date night a priority when it seems impossible, that is what we do.

And this thing I call "mommy guilt" has to go. No way will anyone tell me that taking care of my body, mind, and spirit is selfish or vain.

I can't be the person I was meant to be without depositing back into my own love tank. No one can make you happy if you can't do it for yourself first. It makes so much sense to me now, but at the time, I didn't see what was happening.

Learning from my mistakes and working through these issues with my husband has allowed me to redirect my attention to what really matters in life, being true to myself and passionate about the things that motivate me.

In other words, I released my inner badass!

Now, that I've come full circle, I want the same for you.

HEALTH IS WEALTH

TIFFANY LEE GASTON | FROM BROKEN TO BADASS

HEALTH IS WEALTH

In attempting to change my body the wrong way over the years, I've learned I first needed to alter my mindset. In learning how to help correct a distorted body image, something I occasionally still find myself struggling with, I've learned a lot about the correct way to care for myself. Often times, self-acceptance is at the heart of our struggles.

When we compare ourselves to others, we are unfairly and unknowingly setting ourselves up for failure. My younger self disliked the muscles on my body, never appreciating how very capable they were in performing like an athlete. When you watch an engine work, you appreciate how each component contributes to the functionality of the whole.

Why then do we focus on big thighs or thick waists? Because we are looking at images of others, some of which aren't even their own reality, and we are striving to be just like them.

Distance yourself from your body, just for a moment. Step back and take a look at the beautiful person you are. If your legs are strong and capable, you need to view them as such. If you're built on a muscular frame, embrace it. Find the beauty in the attributes you have and let go of what others possess.

Discover your unique gifts and release the negative thoughts you carry. If you can't change it, accept it and seek positivity. Set yourself free from the prison you've kept yourself in. What we deem as beautiful or appealing can be different for each of us. The muscular legs I once tried to hide because of the stares and comments I'd get are now my absolute favorite feature. I have learned to love and embrace the way I was intended to be and use it in my favor.

FOOD IS NOT THE ENEMY

It's easy to overcomplicate things where food is concerned.

I should know...

Having competed in many fitness and figure competitions over the years, I've weighed and measured my meals to the nth degree. Not an ounce more or less than the strictly prescribed diet I was on, I executed my obsessive-compulsive disorder in new ways altogether.

I would actually feel guilty if I was over or under my exact portions or couldn't get all of my food in during the day, which was yet another reason I walked away from the sport.

The unhealthy obsession over when my next cheat meal would be, what I would eat and from where, weighed heavily on me all week long. And when it happened, I couldn't stop.

I'd eat until I was nearly sick, not realizing that all of the strictly calculated calories I was consuming, was actually creating a binge disorder.

Great, now I was on the other side of the spectrum. This is not uncommon for women in the sport and I'd discuss this with others and learn they were having the same struggles.

To be so heavily scrutinized on stage for your appearance, you learn to appreciate the precise measurements of what you eat. Without knowing the exact consumption, you are unable to tweak things when your body is no longer responding.

I will never say I won't compete again, but I can say I will never do it the same way. It was very difficult on my family. My moods were all over the place. I was uptight about social situations, if I'd even agree to them, and I was missing out on lots of moments I should've shared with my children.

These days, I thrive on balance and no longer obsess over my food. Since visually learning what a portion should look like, I can eyeball a 4-ounce portion with ease.

I enjoy the simplicity of eating an anti-inflammatory diet. I'm not a fan of labels, but for ease of conversation, I identify most with Paleo.

I've been eating a mostly Paleo diet for over four years now. I don't adhere super strictly to it, as I utilize supplements occasionally out of convenience, and I don't eat tons of red meat, as some believe is typical for this lifestyle.

In simplest terms, I do not eat grains, dairy, or processed foods whenever possible.

What do I eat?

Usually lean proteins like chicken, fish, turkey, bison, or ground beef, along with tons of vegetables, fruits, nuts, and seeds. I eat starchier carbohydrates such as sweet potatoes around a workout and eat lots of low glycemic carbs throughout the day.

I've found that there is no need to highly regulate everything I eat when I simply follow this lifestyle and it's quite easy to find options in most restaurants. It's a great feeling to no longer be a slave to the scale, both in and out of the kitchen.

I've found this to be easily sustainable for my busy schedule. Although I didn't start out with the intention to omit grains from my diet, as I gradually reduced the amount I was eating along with any dairy products, I just felt really good and began to read as much as I could about the Paleo lifestyle.

I aim to eat this way 85-90% of the time, allowing for indulgence when I want, which is typically once or twice a week. Cutting back on the inflammatory foods carries with it a plethora of positive side effects.

Some such benefits are:

- ✔ Improved sleep
- ✔ Improved energy
- ✔ More balanced moods
- ✔ Weight loss
- ✔ Better overall health and wellness

SET GOALS

Set goals for yourself and write them down or create a document on your computer, as I have.

There's just something about sitting down and making a list of things you want to accomplish that makes you take it seriously. It's a good habit to adopt.

Make two lists, as both short term goals and long-term goals are important. If you say something you intend to do and just put it out there, it is a mere wish, hope, or dream, and not something you're holding yourself to account.

Write it down, put it somewhere visible, and read it aloud each day as a reminder of what you're working toward.

Crossing things off your list will give you a great sense of accomplishment!

LEARN TO DEAL WITH NEGATIVE EMOTIONS

Before I decided to become a mother, I knew I would never be ready until I learned to properly handle all of the negative emotions beneath the surface.

For many years, I handled my emotions primarily by displaying anger. I was a hothead, because I knew no other way to express myself.

This created issues with my mother, within my marriage, and caused me to push close friends away. I harbored such anger and resentment for one person, that it ultimately came out in a variety of ways within my own life, and often directed at those I loved.

I regret many situations in which I caused tension and hurt feelings, but I know now that I lacked understanding.

I didn't know why I was lashing out, which only made things worse. But I have come to terms with my actions, taken responsibility, and learned from my mistakes.

Always look for ways to turn negatives into positives. It may take you a while, but with knowledge comes wisdom, and with wisdom comes a way forward.

STOP SELLING YOURSELF SHORT

Don't get down on yourself. There are times you may feel like you've missed your calling and now it's too late to do anything about it. It's never too late to be your best self!

If you've made mistakes in the past, don't dwell on them. Recognize them, learn from them, and then leave them exactly where they are – in the past.

You need to forgive yourself before you can move on, often easier said than done, but time heals all. Forgiveness is the best gift you can give yourself.

Life is your own unique journey. It will ebb and flow and evolve. You are not the same person you were twenty years ago, or even three years or three months ago. Let go of the anger, the hatred, the pain, and anything else rooted to whatever keeps you from being your best self and doing what you are passionate about today.

Right here, right now, in this very moment, you are creating your future self! Let go of the self-doubt, negative thoughts, and naysayers.

Look at me - I've drop kicked my past mistakes and not once have I looked back! Until *now*.

This journey through my past has been very painful. Some of the things I've shared with you are things I've tried not to think about for many years.

Baring my soul and my past pain in this way, has left me with even more hope for the future. I am grateful to have gone through these challenges in life, because I have grown in tremendous ways as a person.

Even now, when I look back on that abusive relationship I endured, it's very difficult for me to stir up that emotion once again. I shudder to think what could've been, had I stayed with him.

There are many who struggle to escape the invisible grip of abuse that do not end up so lucky. Some live their entire lives in desperation or worse, if they don't generate the internal strength to leave.

Abuse is never okay and it must always be known for what it is – a violation of your humanity.

If you are in such a relationship, I hope my story can help you in some small way. If you're not, I hope it raises your awareness, so you can help someone else should you witness the signs.

Sadly, I know many who read this already understand the tragic consequences of abuse. If you're one, please know that I'm on your side, pulling for you every step of the way, whether your trauma is in the past or happening now.

For me, I look back on the words my mother spoke to me at age eleven, and I'm so proud they stuck with me after all these years. Had I not held them closely and used them in a moment of desperation, who knows where I'd be today?

The moment I put my foot down and appreciated my own worth, was the moment my abuser no longer controlled me.

It's never too late to change direction in your life. It's never too late to follow your dreams. If you push yourself harder, your results will change. You must expect more of yourself to get more from yourself.

Make the decision to take better care of yourself and do all that you enjoy in life! Your mind can be the grandest source of negativity or positivity, depending on what you choose to allow.

We all "speak" to ourselves, whether it's out loud in the car when we think no one's watching or that little voice in our head that tells us what to do.

Realize how you speak to yourself and make a conscious effort to shift gears if you are having negative thoughts. Conversely, if someone close to you is putting negative thoughts in your head, you also have a choice to distance yourself from them.

Get away from toxicity! You do not have to take that from anyone. It can be difficult, but if a friend, family member, spouse, boyfriend, or girlfriend brings you down, bring it to their attention. If they ignore your feelings, they do not truly have your best interests at heart.

You do not have to settle for that type of treatment. It's your choice.

Each morning when you wake up, give yourself at least one positive affirmation. One example might be, "I am good enough, I am strong enough, I am beautiful enough just the way I am! I can conquer the world today!"

It may sound silly, but I'm sure you've heard the phrase, 'the power of positive thinking.' There is great power in positive thoughts, and when we say them out loud, we give voice to our aspirations. We tell the world, and ourselves, that we have value.

Pound your chest if you have to, just make a habit to be more aware of your inner voice and the way that *you* speak to *you*.

Treat yourself well, and others will follow your lead.

YOU ARE A BEAUTIFUL BADASS

TIFFANY LEE GASTON | FROM BROKEN TO BADASS

YOU ARE A BEAUTIFUL BADASS

Finding the courage to share my story took a long time, but it has been a freeing and therapeutic experience. There's a great deal of pride associated with digging yourself out of a hole and then looking back at just how far you've come.

Being so young and having the ability to learn from my mistakes, has allowed me to have an even stronger relationship with my husband.

As strange as it sounds, I would not trade my mistakes for anything, because they have led me to where I am today.

I never truly understood forgiveness until I nearly lost everything, because I had never really acknowledged or owned the pain and emotion I was holding on to.

Through the process of writing this book, I'm only just now releasing the last of the emotion I once suppressed. Things I've kept buried over the past eighteen years, have risen to the surface once again, but I am no longer that same broken little girl.

I'm one stubborn girl and I always felt forgiving those who hurt me would allow them off the hook. I see now that when you release the resentment and pain you harbor towards another person, you are not giving them anything. The gift is yours.

I am allowing myself the release of the pain I endured, the time I wasted, and the heartache I experienced, and I'm doing it all for myself.

I give my abuser nothing.

It's not for me to decide, but I do believe karma.

The pain of my past caused me to carry my anger far

too long, and it is a tremendous feeling to unburden myself of all that came before.

I release my past to its proper place and embrace the future.

I no longer worry about what will come; instead I make plans, set goals and look forward to the challenges of each new day. I have faith in knowing all the pieces of my puzzle will eventually fall into place, because of the efforts I put forth daily.

I now believe in myself and my abilities and ultimately in the beauty of my strength. We all have an inner badass, some of us just need to dig a bit deeper to discover it. Some need a gentle nudge to chase after it and bring it to the surface, but never, ever doubt that it lies within us all.

> *"Stop trying so hard and follow your heart. It will always lead you right where you need to be." - TLG*

POST SCRIPT
TIFFANY LEE GASTON | FROM BROKEN TO BADASS

POST SCRIPT

As I read through my work, it is more evident than ever, that my fitness journey began as an outlet for the pain I once suppressed.

Even now, I find therapy in my training. When I'm working out very hard, I go to a place where no one can touch me. I am focused and driven and my mind is clear.

While I am not good at everything, I am hardworking and determined. That said, I also realize I still have an addictive personality.

So if it wasn't drugs or alcohol or an eating disorder, there would probably always be something I would obsess over.

I'm fortunate that a healthy mind and body has become my greatest obsession.

Discovering fitness saved my life.

My greatest mission, however, has become sharing my passion with others to help them also find a better outlet for their feelings.

In the process of your own search for what makes you happiest, you can transform body, mind, and soul and discover an inner strength you never knew you had. That is where I have found myself today, and ultimately what I want for you as well.

Thank you for allowing me to share my story. I hope it has given you some insight, that to each of us, there is so much more than meets the eye.

To all you moms and moms-to-be, please never lose sight of your ability to shine and be the amazing woman you were meant to be. Your children will appreciate your inner badass more than you'll ever know. And to the men, the same goes for you, however, please support your ladies and appreciate that although they may be mothers now, they still have their own passions and desires and support that in any way you can.

I know the support I'm fortunate enough to have in my own life, is something that has enabled me to flourish. I now have a man that loves me for all that I am, and as it turns out, that's all I've ever wanted.

To be celebrated just as you are, is the love we all deserve in life, especially from ourselves.

Having once felt broken, I used my pain to build my strength piece by piece until my inner badass emerged. If I can do it, you can too!

tiffanyleegaston.com

STRONG
FITNESS MAGAZINE
TRAINING GUIDE
EXPERT ADVICE TO FIX SHOULDER PAIN FOR GOOD
your BEST LEG DAY EVER
The workout for a strong lower half
DO-IT-YOURSELF TRIGGER POINT THERAPY
BEAT COLD SEASON
SHOULD YOU TRY CROSSFIT?
LEGS FOR DAYS
NPC NEWS ONLINE
ARE YOUR EMOTIONS DERAILING YOUR FAT-LOSS EFFORTS?
SCULPT SEXY ABS
A COMPLETE 4 STEP GUIDE
GYM GEAR GUIDE
IS THERE A WONDER WEIGHT LOSS PILL?
THE COST OF PROTEIN
MOVES TO BURN MORE CALORIES
STREET WORKOUT
FROM BROKEN TO BADASS
hers
POWER MEALS
FREE!
FLAT-ABS DIET PLAN
BOOST THE BURN
NEW RULES FOR FAT LOSS
WOMEN Be healthy. Be fit. Be you.
MEET OUR FAB 5 COVER GIRL 2015 FINALISTS
Tiffany Gaston's Strong body secrets revealed Steal her workout!
FIGHT FAT AND FEEL HEALTHY!
10 PLANS FOR INTENSE FAT BURNING
FITNESS PROGRAM STALLED?
WHAT YOU NEED TO KNOW ABOUT UNDER-FUELING
Scottsdale HEALTH
STRESS AWARENESS MONTH
April Finds
TIFFANY
CURIOUS ABOUT CHOLESTEROL? GET IN THE KNOW TODAY
YOUR HOLIDAY RESCUE PLAN SORTED!
MEDITATE THE POUNDS AWAY
HARNESS THE POWER OF YOUR MIND
MASTER YOUR KETTLEBELL ROUTINE WHILE STAYING SAFE
Have You Entered the $25K MaxForm Life Challenge?
MAX SPORTS & FITNESS
KILLER FAT BURNERS
SIX-WEEK FAT BLAST
DON'T MISS THIS HARDCORE WORKOUT
6 WAYS TO MAKE YOUR WEIGHT-LOSS PLAN STICK
LEAN CYCLE THREE
Ultimate Weight Loss Stack
REAL RESULTS
MEET TWO MORE 2013 MAXFORM FINALISTS
THE TRUTH ABOUT CALORIES
HEART HEALTH
THE LATEST NEWS & TIPS
FREE ISSUE!
FEBRUARY 2014